E242
EDUCATION: A SECOND-LEVEL COUR

LEARNING FOR ALL

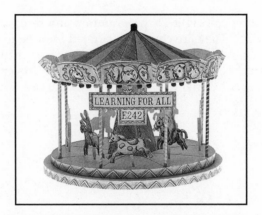

UNIT 5
RIGHT FROM THE START

Prepared for the course team by
Patricia Potts with contributions from
Pat Petrie and June Statham

The Open
University

E242 COURSE READERS

There are two course readers associated with E242; they are:

BOOTH, T., SWANN, W., MASTERTON, M. and POTTS, P. (eds) (1992) *Learning for All 1: curricula for diversity in education*, London, Routledge (**Reader 1**).

BOOTH, T., SWANN, W., MASTERTON, M. and POTTS, P. (eds) (1992) *Learning for All 2: policies for diversity in education*, London, Routledge (**Reader 2**).

TELEVISION PROGRAMMES AND AUDIO-CASSETTES

There are eight TV programmes and three audio-cassettes associated with E242. They are closely integrated into the unit texts and there are no separate TV or cassette notes. However, further information about them may be obtained by writing to Open University Educational Enterprises Ltd, 12 Cofferidge Close, Stony Stratford, Milton Keynes MK11 1BY.

Cover illustration shows a detail from 'Midsummer Common' by Dorothy Bordass.

The Open University, Walton Hall, Milton Keynes MK7 6AA

First published 1992. Reprinted 1994

Copyright © 1992 The Open University

Designed by the Graphic Design Group of The Open University

Typeset by The Open University

Printed in Scotland by Thomson Litho Ltd, East Kilbride

ISBN 0 7492 6107 2

This unit forms part of an Open University course; the complete list of units is printed at the end of this book. If you have not enrolled on the course and would like to buy this or other Open University material, please write to Open University Educational Enterprises Ltd, 12 Cofferidge Close, Stony Stratford MK11 1BY, United Kingdom. If you wish to enquire about enrolling as an Open University student, please write to the Admissions Office, The Open University, PO Box 48, Walton Hall, Milton Keynes MK7 6AB, United Kingdom.

1.2

CONTENTS

1 INTRODUCTION

1.1   In this unit we argue that the complexity, instability and regional variability of services for pre-school children lead to inequalities in the experiences of young children and their families. Within the current framework, parents may have access to specialist services but they only rarely have the choice of an appropriate service provided in a more comprehensive setting.

1.2   One of the reasons why provision for pre-school children is so complicated is that there are very different value-systems underlying the various forms. For example, nursery education is seen to be a good thing, but only if it is part-time and does not take children out of their family context for long periods. Non-parental childcare is still seen by many as a necessary evil, to be provided for children classified as being 'in need', but not to be provided for every child whose family wants it. Families and service providers may have very different perspectives on what should be the aims and characteristics of pre-school provisions.

1.3   There is a range of arguments in favour of making provision for pre-school children but they are not necessarily compatible nor the reflection of a policy based on children's rights. Here are five such reasons:

- experience of a pre-school group can be seen as a useful preparation for entering full-time education later;

- pre-school experience can be seen as socially beneficial in itself;

- when children attend a pre-school group, their parents are able to work outside the home;

- membership of a pre-school group can provide respite from and possible alleviation of social and other kinds of problems;

- pre-school experience can stimulate the overall development of the children, with long-lasting advantages.

These arguments reflect the interests, not only of children and their parents, but also of educators, psychologists, social workers, employers and politicians.

1.4   In this unit we examine the ways in which the views of parents and their young children are or are not supported by the professionals and others from whom they receive services, and explore the debates and dilemmas that arise in connection with making provision for children before they go to school.

1.5   As part of this unit we shall ask you to read or watch and discuss the following as you work through Section 4, 'Integrating children and services'.

Readings

Reader 2, Chapter 8: 'Attempting to integrate under fives: policy in Islington, 1983–8' by Margaret Boushel, Claire Debenham, Lisa Dresner and Anna Gorbach.

Reader 2, Chapter 9: 'Community play' by Veronica Hanson. This article describes how children with widely varying abilities and interests are being included in ordinary playgroups in Wales.

Reader 2, Chapter 7: 'Provision for the under fives: bringing services together' by Kathryn Riley.

Television Programme 2

Learning to Care is a study of policy and practice in the Scottish region of Strathclyde in the late 1980s, when a new Pre-Five Unit set out to unify services within the education department.

2   PRE-SCHOOL PROVISION IN THE UNITED KINGDOM

2.1   In the United Kingdom the variety of childcare, play and educational services for under-fives is bewildering. A cursory glance at the range of provision – private, public, voluntary, charitable and commercial – demonstrates that there is no clear agreement about what is necessary and desirable, and certainly no central government commitment to public provision. In this section we look at the range of provision for children under five and at the legislative framework for services introduced by the Children Act (1989).

FAMILIES NEED RESOURCES

2.2   The legal responsibility for the care of children lies with parents but they do not have to carry out all the work themselves nor rely solely on their own material resources. Some families use private services but most parents depend upon public services.

2.3   Local authority nursery schools and day nurseries are discretionary. Authorities are under no obligation to provide them, although they are obliged, under the terms of the Children Act, to provide care for children 'in need' (see the discussion of the Children Act later in this section). The Act is to be implemented in October 1991, at the time this unit was being written, and it remains to be seen how this will influence the pattern of pre-school provision. The lack of legal obligation in the United Kingdom has meant that public provision is relatively scarce in comparison with the rest of Europe.

Activity 1   The European league table

Look at Table 1 (overleaf). It shows the number of places in publicly funded childcare services in member states of the European Community (Moss, 1990, p. 10).

Rank the different countries as to the number of places for children under the age of three.

Then do the same for each year from the age of three to the age when compulsory schooling starts. You can see from the table that this varies from country to country. Note also that in the United Kingdom many of the publicly funded places for over-threes are occupied by four-year-olds in primary schools.

Are you surprised by what you find?

A JIGSAW OF SERVICES

2.4   The lack of public provision explains some, but not all, of the variety among the services which do exist. Different services have their own histories and objectives; they employ staff from a range of professional backgrounds, as well as untrained workers and volunteers. They are governed by different and sometimes conflicting strands of social policy.

2.5   All provision, public, private and voluntary, can include children with widely varying abilities and children have a legal right to pre-school educational services if they are formally identified and assessed under the terms of the 1981 Education Act.

Private provision

2.6   Private services for under-fives outside the home include childminders and private nurseries. All have to be registered with and inspected by the local authority. The background of staff varies: some are untrained, others may have attended a childminding or a Pre-School Playgroups Association (PPA) course, some may have a diploma or certificate from the Business and Technical Education Council (BTEC) or the National Nursery Examination Board (NNEB) and others may be professionally trained teachers or nurses.

Table 1 Places in publicly funded childcare services as a percentage of all children in the age group.

	Date to which data refer	For children under 3	For children from 3 to compulsory school age	Age when compulsory schooling begins	Length of school day (including midday break)	Outside school-hours care for primary school children
Germany	1987	3%	65–70%	6–7 years	4–5 hours (a)	4%
France	1988	20%	95%+	6 years	8 hours	?
Italy	1986	5%	85%+	6 years	4 hours	?
Netherlands	1989	2%	50–55%	5 years	6–7 hours	1%
Belgium	1988	20%	95%+	6 years	7 hours	?
Luxembourg	1989	2%	55–60%	5 years	4–8 hours (a)	1%
United Kingdom	1988	2%	35–40%	5 years	$6\frac{1}{2}$ hours	(–)
Ireland	1988	2%	55%	6 years	$4\frac{1}{2}$–$6\frac{1}{2}$ hours (b)	(–)
Denmark	1989	48%	85%	7 years	3–$5\frac{1}{2}$ hours (a,b)	29%
Greece	1988	4%	65–70%	$5\frac{1}{2}$ years	4–5 hours (b)	(–)
Portugal	1988	6%	35%	6 years	$6\frac{1}{2}$ hours	6%
Spain	1988	?	65–70%	6 years	8 hours	(–)

NB. This table should be read in conjunction with the national reports, which contain important qualifications and explanations. The table shows the number of *places* in *publicly funded* services as a percentage of the child population; the percentage of *children* attending may be higher because some places are used on a part-time basis. Provision at playgroups in the Netherlands has not been included, although 10% of children under 3 and 25% of children aged 3–4 attend and most playgroups receive public funds. Average hours of attendance – 5–6 hours per week – are so much shorter than for other services, that it would be difficult and potentially midleading to include them on the same basis as other services; however, playgroups should not be forgotten when considering publicly funded provision in the Netherlands.

Key: ? = no information; (–) = less than 0.5%; (a) = school hours vary from day to day; (b) = school hours increase as children get older.

(Source: Moss, 1990, p. 10)

Childminders

2.9   Childminders provide most of the non-parental childcare for parents
who are employed outside the home; the equivalent, taking into account
part-time arrangements, of places for 5 per cent of all children under five
(Moss, 1990). Childminders look after children in their own, not the
children's, homes. Some are happy to welcome children with disabilities
or who experience other kinds of difficulty. A few are employed or
sponsored by their local authority, but most childminders work privately.

Private nurseries

2.10   Private nurseries are owned by commercial or voluntary
organizations (for example, Barnado's or the National Children's Home)
and provide places for 1 per cent of under-fives (Moss, 1990). Children
may attend on a full-time or a part-time basis. Some nurseries take
babies, but most do not. Some aim to provide education for the children,
as well as care. One form of private nursery is the community nursery,
set up and run by parents and others in the local area. Another is the
company nursery, provided for employees. These are not common.

2.11   There was much publicity in the late 1980s and early 1990s about
the need to attract mothers back into the workforce (National Economic
Development Organization, 1989) and as a result many private
individuals and companies considered setting up nurseries to meet
employees' childcare needs. Although some got off the ground, many
schemes did not get past the planning stage (Whittingham, 1991).
Partnerships between local authorities, voluntary organizations and
employers may be one way to set up high-quality daycare which has
guaranteed funding and experienced workers and managers (Hogg,
Kozak and Petrie, 1989).

Voluntary provision

Playgroups

2.7   The Pre-School Playgroups Association has, for more than
twenty-five years, promoted opportunities for play not available at home:
space, safe conditions, toys and other equipment, and the company of
other children. There are now numerous play associations, including a
National Playbus Association. The Handicapped Adventure Playground
Association (HAPA) was formed in 1970 to promote play opportunities
for children with disabilities and currently there are moves towards
integrated play provision.

2.8   Playgroups are attended by about 50 per cent of all three- and
four-year-olds, usually on a part-time basis. Parents are involved in their
management and in helping with the play sessions on a rota system.

Local authority provision

2.12   Local authorities have the right to provide nurseries, family centres
and education for children under five. However, for children 'in need',
this right becomes a duty.

Social services provision

2.13   Less than 2 per cent of pre-school children attend local authority day nurseries or family centres. Usually they are children who are seen as being 'in need', for example, those who might otherwise be taken into full-time local authority care. Places are allocated according to a system of priorities. In the case of family centres, additional support may be available for parents; for example, advice sessions, counselling, support groups, childcare classes.

Local education authority provision

2.14   Although local education authorities have no statutory obligations towards children under five, most of them see pre-school education as valuable in itself and as a foundation for the development of children's later learning (see Section 5). Children are admitted to nursery schools or classes from the age of three and 25 per cent of three- and four-year-olds attend these provisions. However, 20 per cent of this group are four-year-olds in the reception classes of primary schools.

2.15   A qualified teacher will be appointed to be in charge of a nursery class and has an assistant, another teacher or a qualified nursery nurse, working alongside. Teachers may also work in social services day nurseries and family centres, but these are usually staffed by workers who have done a two-year training, post-sixteen, like the NNEB or BTEC courses.

Segregated pre-school provision

2.16   Many special schools have nursery classes and they can admit children from the age of two, younger than they would be admitted to an ordinary nursery class. Some special schools expanded their nursery provision during the 1980s. In some areas, therefore, specialist resources for pre-school children have been concentrated in segregated settings, despite the encouragement of the 1981 Education Act to support young children within ordinary groups and despite the fact that there seems to be no clear policy for deciding which children should be referred to a segregated provision.

2.17   Following her review of placement decisions across the United Kingdom for under-fives with disabilities or other kinds of difficulties, Brenda Robson (1989) concluded that:

> Even within a local authority there is no rationale governing decisions to place children in ordinary or special provision. On the whole, children in ordinary facilities would fall within the sphere of moderate to minimal special needs on a continuum of severity while the most severely disabled children were found in special nursery classes. There is considerable overlap, however, and a broad grey area in the middle where children could be placed in either category.
> (Robson, 1989, p. 30)

2.18   The advantage of having a wide range of specialist support, materials and equipment to hand in a special school is counter-balanced by the diversity of the children's ages, which could be as high as ten, and the particularity of their individual needs in the absence of an ordinary mix: 'The range of children placed in a nursery class meant that for many children there was no real peer group stimulation to encourage cognitive and linguistic development and social skills' (Robson, 1989, p. 31).

Funding

2.19   Some services are resourced from public or charitable funds, others scratch together what they can from jumble sales and other fund-raising to supplement parental contributions, while childminders and commercial nurseries charge fees.

2.20   The areas with the most pre-school education provision are those where the local authorities spend most. They also tend to coincide with areas where there is greater material disadvantage. But the amount of money which local authorities spend on services for under-fives is affected by central government policy towards public spending, as well as by decisions taken locally.

Local variations

2.21   Look at Figures 1 and 2 (on page 12). The maps show the number of places for under-fives in two different sorts of provision: nursery education and playgroups. These are the most common forms of provision for three- and four-year-olds in England. In 1986, some 40–50 per cent of these children attended pre-school playgroups and about 22 per cent were in public nursery schools. The maps indicate how many places were available per thousand children under the age of five in English local authorities. The darker the shading, the higher the number of places.

2.22   You can see that there is a great deal of variation. The shading does not, in fact, convey all of it. For example, Gloucester, Somerset, Wiltshire and Bromley provide six or fewer education places per thousand under-fives. (See also Table 2, p. 13.) Also, the higher the level of public provision, the lower the private; and vice versa. It looks as if playgroups are 'chosen' by parents when in fact there may be no public provision in their area or no system for distributing adequate information about existing services.

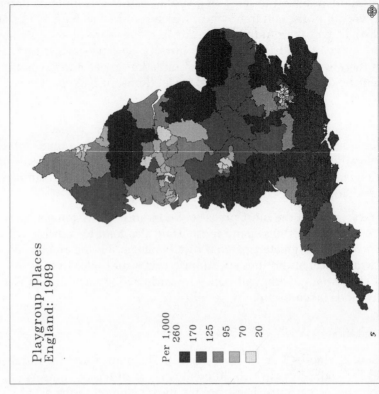

Playgroup Places
England: 1989

Per 1,000
260
170
125
95
70
20

Figure 2 Playgroup places in England, 1989 (from information provided by the Thomas Coram Research Unit).

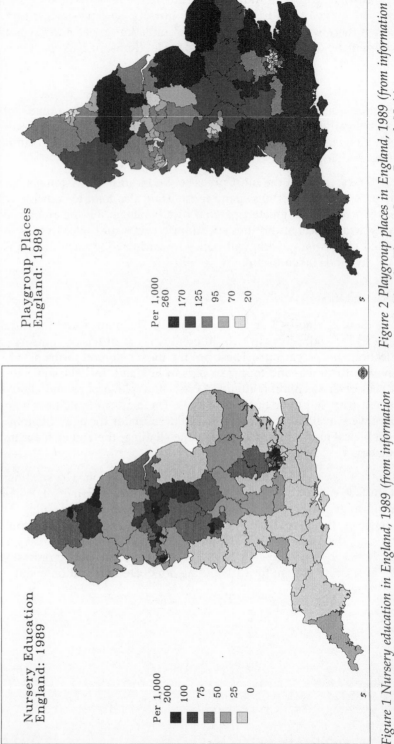

Nursery Education
England: 1989

Per 1,000
200
100
75
50
25
0

Figure 1 Nursery education in England, 1989 (from information provided by the Thomas Coram Research Unit).

Table 2 Variation between levels of provision among LEAs in England, 1987.

Nursery school and class places (numbers of children attending Jan. 1987 as a percentage of the 3- and 4-year-old population)	All under-five places	Playgroup places (number of places Mar. 1986 as a percentage of the 0–4-year-old population)
Top four:		
1 Hounslow 66%	Walsall 92%	Bromley 24%
2 Walsall 59%	S Tyneside 87%	W Sussex 24%
3 Wolverhampton 58%	N Tyneside 87%	Gloucestershire 22%
4 Newham 56%	Salford 83%	Surrey 22%
Bottom four:		
1 Gloucestershire 0%	W Sussex 9%	S Tyneside 2%
2 Somerset 1%	Kent 12%	Newham 3%
3 Wiltshire 2%	Dorset 14%	Doncaster 3%
4 Bromley 2%	Hereford & Worc. ⎫ Oxfordshire ⎬ 16%	Sandwell ⎫ Manchester ⎬ 6% N Tyneside ⎭

Source of figures: DES Statistical Bulletin 4/88 and DHSS 'Children's Day Care Facilities at 31 March 1986'.
(Source: House of Commons Select Committee on Education, Science and Arts, 1989, p. xv)

THE CHILDREN ACT (1989)

2.23   The scope of the Children Act (1989) is vast. It covers children in family proceedings, local authority support for children and families, the protection of children against abuse, children living in homes, fostering, daycare and a host of miscellaneous related matters. The basic principles underlying the Act are that the child's welfare is 'paramount', that all decisions should be taken with this in mind and that the child's or young person's own views and perspectives should be listened to and given weight.

2.24   Part III of the Act places a duty on local authorities:

(a) to safeguard and promote the welfare of children within their area who are in need; and

(b) so far as is consistent with that duty, to promote the upbringing of such children by their families, by providing a range and level of services appropriate to those children's needs.

(Children Act, 1989, Section 17(1))

2.25   You have read the Act's definition of 'need' in Unit 1/2 and will have seen that it includes disability. You will also have noticed the emotive and medical use of 'suffers', 'deformity' and 'handicapped' (Unit 1/2, paras 3.79–3.80).

2.26   Local authorities have to take 'reasonable steps' to identify the numbers of children in need in their area and they have to publish information about the relevant services that they and other organizations provide (see Schedule 2 of the Act). Every local authority also has to 'open and maintain a register of disabled children within their area' (Schedule 2, Part I, para. 2(1)) and to provide services designed:

(a) to minimise the effect on disabled children within their area of their disabilities; and

(b) to give such children the opportunity to lead lives which are as normal as possible.

(Schedule 2, Part I, para. 6)

2.27   A commitment to the integration of children with disabilities is spelled out in the section of the Guidance and Regulations issued alongside the Act which refers to children under five:

Generally the development of young children with disabilities or special educational needs is more likely to be enhanced through attending a day care service for under fives used by all children. Policy workers, registration officers, providers and practitioners need to consider the means whereby this aim might be achieved in discussion with experts in the field such as health professionals and people working for relevant voluntary organisations. In making arrangements for integrating children with disabilities with other children in a day care or pre-school education setting, particular attention should be paid to the physical environment, staff/child ratios, and training (e.g. in sign language for the profoundly deaf). It may also be desirable for there to be services catering specifically for children with disabilities and special educational needs but these might, with advantage, be attached to a service used by all children so that joint activities can be arranged from time to time.

(Children Act, 1989, Guidance and Regulations, vol. 2, para. 6.8)

2.28   In an article summarizing the main sections of the Children Act, Phillipa Russell refers to 'the seamless service principle, within children's services, of compatible and complementary legislation' (Russell, 1990, p. 37). She concludes that:

The Children Act, 1981 Education Act, 1986 Disabled Persons Act and the NHS Bill, whilst daunting in their present and future duties, also gives teachers and administrators new powers as well as duties to work with children and parents and to ensure that the children with special needs are not seen as part of a separate service but included within mainstream legislation and strategic thinking for the 1990s.

(Russell, 1990, p. 37)

Activity 2   Pre-school services then and now ————————————

Spend a few minutes listing the health, recreational, social, educational and childcare services that you remember making use of from your own pre-school days. Can you remember what you enjoyed and what you disliked?

Now list the services used by children known to you.

Compare your two lists. Have the requirements of young children and their families changed since you yourself were a child? If so, in what way? Are the changes desirable or regrettable?

3   PRE-SCHOOL PROVISION AS EARLY INTERVENTION

3.1   We have just seen that young children with disabilities have the right to pre-school services, such as daycare, if they come within the 1989 Children's Act's definition of 'need'. In Section 5 of this unit you will see how children under five can also secure educational services, despite the fact that pre-school education is non-statutory, by using the terms of the 1981 Education Act. In each Act, there is a commitment to the integration of children with disabilities into non-specialized services, with appropriate additional support. However, there is a range of specialized pre-school services designed to capitalize on the benefits of early intervention.

3.2   In this section the idea of pre-school provision as 'early intervention' is discussed in relation to a home-visiting educational service, to the services provided by medically oriented Child Development Centres and to schemes run by and for parents. We shall ask you to reflect on the possible rationales for these services.

3.3   Services to pre-school children reflect a number of views about the value of early intervention. Some services, for example those designed specifically for children who are experiencing difficulties, may be aiming to reduce or even overcome the children's difficulties, i.e. to be *curative*. Others may see early intervention as *preventive*, and therefore aim to include as wide a range of children as possible. A third view is that all children should receive whatever *support* their families want for them right from the start, irrespective of how long it might be needed, and that services should reflect an acceptance of the ordinariness of disability, which is often neither preventable nor curable. This view rejects the medical model of prevention and cure in favour of a view which is more positive about children as they are.

3.4   It may be that the services illustrated here seem to contain elements of all three of the views outlined above: curative, preventive and supportive. Or it may seem to you that early interventions by health, education or social services cannot hope to prevent, cure or sustain because the children's difficulties require moral and political resolutions which are beyond the reach of practitioners.

PORTAGE: A HOME-VISITING SERVICE

3.5   Portage is a small town in Wisconsin, USA. The 'Portage' home-visiting scheme for pre-school children was developed there by David and Marsha Shearer in the late 1960s as a response to the requirements of the young children in a rural area. The original project was funded by what was then known as the United States Bureau of Education for the Handicapped and was based on the premise that 'parents – with instruction, guidance and support – could teach their own children to grow and develop to their maximum potential' (Shearer and Shearer, 1986, p. ix). The Shearers describe four main features of their model, which would:

> (a) provide comprehensive services to young handicapped children and their families in the child's natural environment – the home, (b) be complex in design yet simple in its implementation, (c) be easily replicated by programs that were without a wide array of human and fiscal resources, and (d) demonstrate that parents from a variety of backgrounds and with a variety of child rearing beliefs could indeed effectively teach their own children.
>
> (Shearer and Shearer, 1986, p. x)

3.6   The first visitors from Portage came to Britain in 1976 and since then schemes have proliferated across the United Kingdom. In 1986 the Department of Education and Science, after two years of discussions with the National Portage Association, agreed to make an Educational Support Grant of £1.2 million to establish Portage schemes in each local education authority. The grants were to be for three years, after which it was hoped that the local authorities would guarantee funding. In the early 1990s, this permanent funding was not forthcoming and consequently many schemes were insecure.

3.7   A series of books about the operation of Portage schemes in the United Kingdom has been published by NFER/Nelson: see Dessent (1984), Daly *et al*. (1985) and Cameron (1986). For an evaluation of one of the earliest Portage schemes in the United Kingdom, the Wessex Portage Project in Hampshire, see Smith, Kushlick and Glossop (1977).

3.8   In *Portage: the importance of parents* (Daly *et al*., 1985), there is a list of eight core elements which characterize Portage home teaching schemes. They are:

1   Families are visited weekly at home by a visitor who has completed a Portage Workshop training.

2   The Portage home visitor attends a regular staff meeting with the project supervisor.

3   A checklist is used for initial and on-going assessment.

4   An *activity chart* consisting of instructions, agreed with the parents, on what to teach, how to teach it and what to record, is left with them each week for each of the skills being taught.

5   The agreed teaching procedure is demonstrated by the home visitor …

6   The home visitor observes the parents carrying out the procedure and offers advice and/or agrees amendments to it.

7   The child's level of skill in the area concerned is recorded both *before* teaching and a week *after* teaching, so that improvements can be measured.

8   There is a management team (of representatives of social services, health, education, voluntary agencies and parents), which meets every three or four months to receive the supervisor's report and deal with related inter-agency or resource issues.

(Daly *et al.*, 1985, Editorial)

Portage materials

3.9   The Portage materials comprise a checklist, activity cards and activity charts. The checklist consists of 580 items which are brief descriptions of a child's behaviour, designed to cover the first six years of a child's life. The checklist is arranged in five separate developmental sequences headed: socialization, language, self-help, cognitive and motor. These sequences are prefaced by an introductory section covering the first six months of life. The checklist is used to establish a child's current stage of development, to identify and encourage a child's 'emerging' skills and to plan a curriculum for future teaching (see Figure 3).

3.10   There is one activity card for every item on the Portage checklist, containing suggestions for how to teach that item (see Figure 4). The examples I have illustrated are cards that were originally published in 1976 but still in use in 1991.

3.11   Activity charts are the documents compiled by the child's parent and the home teacher together. Mollie White, one of the UK's first Portage home teachers, describes the chart as 'without doubt the most important component of the Portage teaching materials' (White, 1986, p. 73). The aim of these structured charts is the weekly achievement of a specified behavioural objective on the part of the child and their main advantage is seen to be their level of individualized detail (see Figure 5).

Portage
Checklist
© CESA 5 and NFER-NELSON

cognitive

Age Levels: 0 – 1 (1 – 14); 1 – 2 (15 – 24); 2 – 3 (25 – 40); 3 – 4 (41 – 64); 4 – 5 (65 – 86); 5 – 6 (87 – 108)

CARD	BEHAVIOUR	ENTRY BEHAVIOUR	DATE ACHIEVED	COMMENTS
1	Removes cloth from face, that obscures vision		/ /	
2	Looks for object that has been removed from direct line of vision		/ /	
3	Removes object from open container by reaching into container		/ /	
4	Places object in container in imitation		/ /	
5	Places object in container on verbal command		/ /	
6	Shakes a sound-making toy on a string		/ /	
7	Puts 3 objects into a container, empties container		/ /	
8	Transfers object from one hand to the other to pick up another object		/ /	
9	Drops and picks up toy		/ /	
10	Finds object hidden under container		/ /	
11	Pushes 3 blocks train style		/ /	
12	Removes circle from form board		/ /	
13	Places round peg in pegboard on request		/ /	
14	Performs simple gestures on request		/ /	
15	Individually takes out 6 objects from container		/ /	
16	Points to one body part, e.g. nose		/ /	
17	Stacks 3 blocks on request		/ /	
18	Matches like objects		/ /	
19	Scribbles		/ /	
20	Points to self when asked 'Where's (name)?'		/ /	
21	Places 5 round pegs in pegboard on request		/ /	
22	Matches objects with picture of same object		/ /	
23	Points to named picture		/ /	
24	Turns pages of book 2 – 3 at a time to find named picture		/ /	
25	Finds specific book on request		/ /	
26	Completes 3 piece formboard		/ /	
27	Names common pictures		/ /	
28	Draws a vertical line in imitation		/ /	
29	Draws a horizontal line in imitation		/ /	
30	Copies a circle		/ /	
31	Matches textures		/ /	
32	Points to big and little on request		/ /	
33	Draws (+) in imitation		/ /	
34	Matches 3 colours		/ /	
35	Places objects in, on and under on request		/ /	
36	Names objects that make sounds		/ /	
37	Puts together 4 part nesting toy		/ /	
38	Names actions		/ /	
39	Matches geometric form with picture of shape		/ /	
40	Stacks 5 or more rings on a peg in order		/ /	
41	Names big and little objects		/ /	
42	Points to 10 body parts on verbal command		/ /	
43	Points to boy and girl on verbal command		/ /	
44	Tells if object is heavy or light		/ /	
45	Puts together 2 parts of shape to make whole		/ /	
46	Tells what happens next in simple, repetitive story		/ /	
47	Repeats finger plays with words and action		/ /	
48	Matches 1 to 1 (3 or more objects)		/ /	
49	Points to long and short objects		/ /	
50	Tells which objects go together		/ /	
51	Counts to 3 in imitation		/ /	
52	Arranges objects into categories		/ /	
53	Draws a V stroke in imitation		/ /	

Figure 3a   Extract from the Portage checklists for cognitive skills (Portage Early Learning Programme Checklist, *1987).*

CARD	BEHAVIOUR	ENTRY BEHAVIOUR	DATE ACHIEVED	COMMENTS
54	Dresses self with help on t-shirts and all fasteners		/ /	
55	Wipes nose when reminded		/ /	
56	Wakes up dry 2 mornings out of 7		/ /	
57	Males urinate in toilet standing up		/ /	
58	Initiates and completes dressing and undressing except fasteners 75% of time		/ /	
59	Does up poppers or hooks on clothing		/ /	
60	Blows nose when reminded		/ /	
61	Avoids common dangers (e.g. broken glass)		/ /	
62	Puts coat on hanger and replaces hanger on low bar with instructions		/ /	
63	Brushes teeth when given verbal instructions		/ /	
64	Puts on mittens		/ /	
65	Unbuttons large buttons on button board or jacket placed on table		/ /	
66	Buttons large buttons on button board or jacket placed on table		/ /	
67	Puts on boots		/ /	
68	Cleans up spills, getting own cloth		/ /	
69	Avoids poisons and all harmful substances		/ /	
70	Unbuttons own clothing		/ /	
71	Buttons own clothing		/ /	
72	Clears place at table		/ /	
73	Puts zip bottom in catch		/ /	
74	Washes hands and face		/ /	
75	Uses correct utensils for food		/ /	
76	Wakes from sleep during night to use toilet or stays dry all night		/ /	
77	Wipes and blows nose 75% of the time when needed without reminders		/ /	
78	Bathes self except for back, neck and ears		/ /	
79	Uses knife for putting soft spreads on toast		/ /	
80	Buckles and unbuckles belt on dress or trousers and shoes		/ /	
81	Dresses self completely, including all front fastenings except ties		/ /	
82	Serves self at table, parent holds serving dish		/ /	
83	Helps set table by correctly placing plates, serviettes and utensils with verbal cues		/ /	
84	Brushes teeth		/ /	
85	Goes to bathroom in time, undresses, wipes self, flushes toilet, and dresses unaided		/ /	
86	Combs or brushes long hair		/ /	
87	Hangs up clothes on hanger		/ /	
88	Goes about neighbourhood without constant supervision		/ /	
89	Laces shoes		/ /	
90	Ties shoes		/ /	
91	Is responsible for one weekly household task and does it on request		/ /	
92	Selects appropriate clothing for temperature and occasion		/ /	
93	Stops at kerb, looks both ways, and crosses street without verbal reminders		/ /	
94	Serves self at table and passes serving dish		/ /	
95	Prepares own cold cereal		/ /	
96	Is responsible for one daily household task (e.g. setting table, taking out rubbish)		/ /	
97	Adjusts water temperature for shower or bath		/ /	
98	Prepares own sandwich		/ /	
99	Walks to school, playground, or shop near home independently		/ /	
100	Cuts soft foods with knife (e.g. sausages, bananas, baked potato)		/ /	
101	Finds correct toilet in public place		/ /	
102	Open ½ pint milk carton		/ /	
103	Picks up, carries, sets down cafeteria tray		/ /	
104	Ties hood strings		/ /	
105	Fastens own seat belt in car		/ /	

Figure 3b   Extract from the Portage checklist for self-help skills (Portage Early Learning Programme Checklist, *1987*).

cognitive 4

AGE 0-1

TITLE: Places object in container in imitation

WHAT TO DO:

1. Say "in," "Put it in" to the child. Reward and praise, smile and hug child, when he does put the object into the container.
2. Physically help child place object in container. Hug and praise child for each object placed in container. Gradually withdraw aid.
3. Use objects that will make a noise when dropped or placed into container (jingle bells, marbles) or fill container with water so that an object splashes when dropped into it.

self help 42

AGE 2-3

TITLE: Places coat on hook placed at child's height

WHAT TO DO:

1. Sew a metal chain in a semi-circle onto the inside of the collar of his coat. Have the child take hold of this and hang it over a hook the child can reach.
2. Practice hanging pot holders with loops over the hook. Begin with a large loop sewn inside child's coat and gradually reduce size to normal.
3. Practice activity when it is functional. When child comes in from outdoors with coat on, have him hang it up.
4. Put name or animal sticker by hook so child knows that it is his special place to hang his coat.

Figure 4   Portage activity cards (Portage Guide, 1976, Co-operative Educational Service Agency)

Checklist number   12

Child's name   Ellen

Home Teacher's name   Annette

Week of   7.12.82

BEHAVIOUR   Ellen will turn her eyes and head in direction of sound.

CRITERIA

   6/6 trials

NUMBER OF   Times Ellen turns eyes and head in direction of sound

	TU	WE	TH	FR	SA	SU	MO
6	(✓)L	(✓)L	✓L	✓L	✓L	✓L	✓L
5	✓R	✓	(✓)R	(✓)R	✓R	(✓)R	✓R
4	(✓)L	(✓)L	✓L	✓L	✓L	✓L	✓L
3	✓R	✓R	✓R	(✓)R	✓R	(✓)R	✓R
2	✓L	(✓)L	✓L	✓L	✓L	✓L	✓L
1	✓R	✓R	✓R	(✓)R	✓R	✓R	✓R

DIRECTIONS   Lie Ellen on the floor on her back. Use a rattle, bell, tissue paper, anything that makes a noise. Hold the noise maker to either side of her and shake or rattle it. Make sure it is loud enough for her to hear. Say "Ellen look". When she turns towards the sound praise her saying "good girl" and smiling. Randomly make sounds in different places and gradually increase the distance between the sound source and Ellen.

REINFORCEMENT   Say "Good girl" and smile

CORRECTION PROCEDURE   If Ellen needs help to find the sound, gently move her head towards the sound.

RECORD   When Ellen turns towards the sound on her own, mark that with ✓ on the chart. If you need to give her help then mark trial on the chart (✓)

   Mark R or L next to the task dependent on whether Ellen turned her eyes and head to right or left.

Figure 5 An activity chart for a very young child (adapted from Jordan and Wolfendale, 1986, p. 15).

3.12   I talked to some parents whose children have had a Portage home teacher, one of whom is also now a home teacher herself. She works in an area where the Portage scheme was set up in 1981 and is run by the local Schools Psychological Service. She is one of two full-time Portage workers and they each see about thirteen children. Additionally, six volunteers work with one family each. The focus is on children aged from 0 to 3. From her perspective as a Portage worker, she describes the kinds of problems that can arise. For example, although she receives referrals direct from the local health visitors, this is not always the case. Sometimes the Child Development Centre, which is run by the health authority, channels referrals, so that delays may occur and a selection process may be introduced. The clinical team may say, 'What do you want to see her for?' if a child seems to have severe disabilities or they may be of the view that 'the mother isn't up to it'. In this way, a medical service can control a service that is designed to be educational. From her perspective as a parent and a consumer of the service, however, she is extremely positive about the experience. In particular, she remembers the way in which the Portage approach validated her view of her child and what a support this was. She also sees the approach as one which is clear, flexible, constructive and an active confirmation of what her daughter could, rather than could not, do.

3.13   Another mother I talked to describes her experience of Portage in terms of the emotional support that the relationship between herself and the home teacher provided, a support that is absent from the intermittent and distant contacts that families routinely have with other professionals. For this mother, her home teacher was like a 'key worker', but more informal, as their friendship grew out of the weekly visits. She went so far as to say, 'If your Portage worker is good, you don't need anybody else.'

3.14   I asked her about two features of the Portage system that worried me: first, the apparent need for there to be at least one parent not in full-time employment and, secondly, a cultural bias in favour of European and North American social customs. She acknowledged that it would have been difficult if she had been in full-time employment when her son was receiving home teaching, just as it is difficult, if not impossible, for parents to go out to work if their children are frequently required to attend clinics and assessment centres, but she says that, for her, this time was so valuable that she has no regrets. She added that, in her area, some day nursery staff have been trained as Portage workers, so that they can work with children who are not at home during the day.

3.15   As far as the cultural bias of the activity cards is concerned, my friend said that, though she had noticed this herself, it would not necessarily amount to a negative discrimination against families from different cultural backgrounds because, in her experience, parents and home teachers do not stick closely to the original cards but write their activity charts much more flexibly, recording present behaviour and the next objective with an actual, rather than a typical, child in mind. Home teachers may not even bring the box of official activity cards with them on their visits.

3.16   In a resource book produced by MENCAP's Under Fives Project, a kind of detailed action plan written from the point of view of parents, Portage schemes are described in positive terms: 'early intervention programmes, such as Portage, enable, rather than disable, parents' (Cameron and Sturge-Moore, 1990, p. 69). Parents are actively involved in the teaching of their children and so they become 'better informed; more realistic about their child's potential and needs; able to make more informed decisions about their child's future; more confident to return to work' (Cameron and Sturge-Moore, 1990, p. 69). Parents are involved as managers of the Portage schemes and their home teacher can act as a link between them and the range of statutory agencies.

Activity 3   Bridges or ladders?

David and Marsha Shearer reflect on the value of the original Portage project in this way:

> Portage Wisconsin, like most other 'Portages' in the world, received its name because it was a place which was a crossover, or portage, from a body of water to land. The name of the town was also a reflection of the project's basic mission. It was designed to serve as a bridge, a way of transferring skills and knowledge from professionals to parents; a way of bridging the gap between deficits exhibited by young children to skills needed for success in a school setting; a crossover from home to school.
>
> (Shearer and Shearer, 1986)

Spend a few minutes looking in detail at this passage. Make a note of what seem to you to be the significant points.

Parents who support Portage have two main reasons for doing so. First, they see the Portage approach as positive, one which validates their feelings about and understandings of their children and which sets up a flexible, constructive and clear teaching and learning relationship. Second, they have experienced vital emotional support for themselves from the regular and informal visits of their Portage workers. They may therefore have felt more confident to participate more effectively in services provided for their children.

Some parents have criticisms of the Portage approach but these do not detract from their overall enthusiasm, and they believe that the problems can be solved. Parents may criticize medical services for controlling referrals to local Portage schemes but they do not seem to feel that the Portage approach itself has to do with making up for the 'deficits' mentioned by the Shearers.

What seem to you to be the main aims of Portage-style projects from the materials you have read so far?

3.17   The Shearers describe a bridge, but a bridge that does not link like with like as horizontal bridges usually do, but one which links deficient young children to successful school students, a reaching down rather than a reaching across, so that children could, as far as they were able, catch up and achieve normality.

3.18   Portage schemes are described very positively by many families, particularly because of the focus on what their children can do. Yet the checklist is based on assumptions about universal norms of behaviour and one of the main aims of the teaching programme is to work on 'behaviours which occur earlier in the sequence than the child's current skill level and which are missing from the child's repertoire' (*Portage Early Education Programme Checklist*, 1987, Introduction). These are known as the child's 'skill deficits'. The use of the yardstick of 'normal' child development inevitably brings with it these negative comparisons, which seem to me to undermine the joy of watching children making progress in their own way.

3.19   So, what purposes are served by Portage home teaching schemes? Here is my list:

- Maximizing the learning potential of individual children.
- Reducing the disruptive behaviour of children.
- Providing emotional support for parents.
- Providing a service for young children in areas where there are no other appropriate services.
- Providing a cost-effective service.
- Providing new roles for educational psychologists.
- Providing a bridge between home and school.
- Providing a link between families and the major service agencies.

How far does my list overlap with your own?

CHILD DEVELOPMENT CENTRES

3.20   Child Development Centres provide health and community services to children in their areas, from birth to school-leaving age. The emphasis is on a multi-disciplinary approach, but CDCs are primarily medical in orientation and usually funded by health authorities. The main functions of a CDC are the care of and co-ordination of provision for children who are referred for 'developmental delay'. Initially, this will involve the detailed assessment of the child's capabilities and state of health.

Tower Hamlets

3.21   The information leaflet of the Tower Hamlets Health Authority's Community Health Service Child Development Unit lists 23 members of its Child Development Team:

6 Bangladeshi parent advisers	1 senior Portage worker
1 parent adviser co-ordinator	1 secretary
1 Bangladeshi interpreter	1 administrator
1 senior occupational therapist	3 child psychiatrists
1 senior speech therapist	1 consultant paediatric neurologist
1 senior physiotherapist	1 community consultant paediatrician
1 social worker	
1 specialist health visitor	2 senior clinical medical officers

3.22   The leaflet states that the team prefers referrals to be made directly by a doctor, or with a doctor's consent if made by someone else. The assessment process is described in this way: a first meeting with the child and parents at an assessment playgroup, two further meetings, then a medical examination by the paediatrician. After this, a 'management plan' is drawn up and implemented if parents agree. This provision is reviewed after three or four months and then kept under review until 'the problem is resolved, the child leaves school or moves out of the district'. Reviews are held not only in the health clinic but also in the day nurseries and the special schools.

3.23   The team wants to be seen as a resource for other professional workers in the area and the specialist health visitor keeps files of information on local voluntary and self-help groups.

3.24   The Tower Hamlets Child Development Team was set up in the 1970s by a consultant paediatrician at the London hospital who had himself been a general practitioner. Children were no longer to queue up to see the doctor in the hospital's out-patients' department but were to be seen by a multi-disciplinary team in a generic children's department where there would be more time for each appointment. Referrals were encouraged from health visitors and the idea was that the team would be as peripatetic as possible.

Wandsworth

3.25   In Wandsworth, the Mary Sheridan Centre provides a rather different pattern of provision. This centre was set up in 1982 to assess pre-school children who were seen to have, or to be likely to have, 'special needs'. The centre is jointly funded by the local health, education and social services and incorporates a nursery class. The centre is open only during term-time, with the following eight members of staff:

1 secretary	1 physiotherapist
1 educational psychologist	1 nursery teacher
1 specialist health visitor	1 nursery assistant
1 speech therapist	1 social worker

The psychologist, teacher, social worker and health visitor are all members of the multi-disciplinary district handicap team, to which the centre is accountable on matters of policy.

3.26   The assessment at the Mary Sheridan Centre is carried out on a continuous basis, with the child and a parent attending the morning nursery class together for a two- to four-week block placement. Giving confidence and support to parents is a joint priority for the centre, alongside the assessment of the children's individual needs:

> Many of the children are initially referred because of language delay or disorder and a significant proportion of children have mothers who are themselves depressed and communicate little with their children, or come from single parent disadvantaged homes where there has been little opportunity for spontaneous stimulation and play.
>
> (ILEA, 1985, Appendix 2.4, pp. 222–3)

3.27   One mother I talked to felt ambivalent about Child Development Centres. On the one hand, referral to a CDC can come as a relief if it heralds an end to uncertainty and the beginning of doing something constructive. On the other hand, the assessment process itself can be extremely stressful. Support for parents is by no means automatic and varies from centre to centre. When her son was born, my friend avoided early assessments; she did not want any premature negative labelling and she did not believe that a predominantly medical approach was appropriate. She did want positive support, however, and she is in favour of multi-disciplinary teamwork. But she sees that, in practice, this teamwork often consists of territorial battles between the specialists who belong to the 'team', who fight over the ownership of a child and who are not in a position to provide for families in a positive way, without seeing the whole family as 'patients'.

3.28   This mother knows that some CDCs can be a lifeline in areas where there are very few services and that some do try to involve parents at every stage of their child's assessment. But if a CDC does provide a good service, then a number of other problems can arise. For example, if a centre is seen locally as excellent, it can easily become the inappropriate focus for other pre-school services, thus extending medical control to services which should be run by other kinds of community professionals or even by parents themselves. My friend would have liked her local CDC to refer children to an opportunity group, where they could have the experience of being in an integrated setting, but it was reluctant to let go of families in this way. A CDC may provide a wide range of services that families do need, but it is unlikely to share control with those families or help them to establish contacts with non-specialist groups. One solution, she suggests, would be to appoint a generic community development worker to act as a bridge for families between the specialist and the community based services. Then families would be put in touch with the ordinary range of provisions offered to any other family, without forfeiting their receipt of specialist support.

3.29   Some doctors have been taking a critical look at these issues. *Health for All Children: a programme for child health surveillance* (Hall, 1989) is the report of a joint working party which included members from the British

Paediatric Association, the General Medical Services Committee of the British Medical Association, the Health Visitors' Association, the Royal College of General Practitioners, the Royal College of Nursing and two additional invited members. The report recommends a reduction in the number of routine screening tests and an increase in the involvement of parents in the shared care of their children.

3.30 The working party acknowledges that the routine examination of children for the purpose of detecting 'developmental impairments' does not make much sense when these very 'impairments' are impossible to define precisely and the examination is therefore of little diagnostic value: 'There is no precise age at which failure to achieve a certain milestone can be said to be abnormal. Whatever cut-off point may be selected for screening purposes, many normal children will fail the test while some with significant problems will pass' (Hall, 1989, p. 73). Social and cultural factors are suggested as more relevant indicators: 'It is possible that the extent to which opportunities for play and learning are available in the child's home might be a more relevant criterion when considering the need for early intervention, rather than the actual level of the developmental attainment' (Hall, 1989, pp. 73–4).

3.31 As far as parents are concerned, moreover, the working party accepts that:

> the majority of parents now expect a different kind of relationship with their professional advisers. They want to be involved in decisions regarding their children's developmental problems and they do not necessarily benefit from a purely medical approach, which perceives developmental delays and impairments as a form of pathology that requires treatment. They nevertheless value guidance on how to handle such difficulties in the most constructive way possible, while avoiding the use of stigmatising labels.
>
> (Hall, 1989, p. 76)

3.32 Yes, but this is easier said than done. You will remember from Unit 3/4 Simon Dyson's account of the impotence of the specialists in the face of parents' requests for support for problems which they saw as ordinary in kind but burdensome in amount. Dyson found that the doctors resorted to making denigrating and irrelevant judgements about parents and their lifestyles of a sort that this working party seems sensitive to and wants to avoid.

3.33 In the preface to the report, the working party hints that guidance can be provided by more than one kind of professional:

> We have deliberately avoided the question of which professionals should carry out the various tasks we have specified. It will be clear from our report that we consider the acquisition of appropriate knowledge, attitudes and skills, and the formation of a constructive relationship with the family, to be more important than the individual's original professional background.
>
> (Hall, 1989, p. ix)

3.34   In acknowledging that developmental examinations are not necessarily useful, that parents have a right to be fully involved in decisions about their children and that a range of professionals can share tasks, this working party would seem to be challenging the automatic medical dominance of pre-school services for children with disabilities or who experience other kinds of difficulty. Perhaps you will be encouraged to undertake an investigation into provision in your own area and discover how far practice in your local CDC resembles that recommended in this report.

PARENT-TO-PARENT SCHEMES

3.35   In Unit 3/4, you read 'Supportive parents for special children' (Reader 2, Chapter 17). You have read, too, one mother's observation that professionals can find it hard to let go of the families with whom they have been working and so fail to provide parents with information on the full range of other services available locally, which can include groups run for and by parents themselves. This view is confirmed by the authors of the MENCAP Under Fives Project resource book *Ordinary Everyday Families ... a human rights issue*:

> Some parents may be satisfied with one individual's view and support, but many feel the need to ask for support beyond the professional network. If they seek out this support for themselves, they often feel angry and resentful at not having been put in touch before. There is still considerable professional concern and anxiety about parents' need to meet in order to share experiences and to support each other at times of need. The 'holding on' to families by professionals should be questioned.

(Cameron and Sturge-Moore, 1990, p. 67)

3.36   Yet parents can offer each other many things that professionals cannot. For example:

- Parents have a twenty-four-hours-a-day experience and understanding of disability; they will often know more than some professionals about their children's problems.

- Parents have first-hand experience of a wider range of services than most professionals.

- Parents are available outside office hours and they are community based.

- Parents can offer each other a once-off meeting or a continuing, closer relationship, a range of alternatives to choose from that is not usually possible with professionals.

3.37   Parents have told me that they get together because they can understand each other in ways that professionals probably cannot. They have shared exceptional experiences, which may have been extremely stressful. However, this source of support may itself be fragile, because of the additional demands made on people whose own lives may be very difficult and exhausting. Also, such schemes can perpetuate a separate, secret world and so may contribute to the further rejection of these families from the mainstream. One solution is for parents to have the same opportunities as other parents of young children to meet each other and get together as they wish. Opportunity groups, pre-school playgroups where a wide diversity of children is welcomed, are a good model of how a similar diversity of parents can be supportive to each other, independently of professionals.

3.38   Another way for parent-to-parent groups to gain strength is for there to be some organized support, perhaps from a relevant voluntary organization, for those experienced parents who find themselves playing a counselling role. One example of this is the Parent Support Link Scheme, based at the KIDS Family Centre in Camden, London: 'Parent-to-Parent schemes work best alongside a structure which carefully matches families according to their children's age and special needs, but which also recognises the needs of the befriending parents' (Cameron and Sturge-Moore, 1990, p. 68).

3.39   The KIDS Scheme was devised by Naomi Dale, the director of the centre and a psychologist. She runs courses for parent befrienders, the objectives of which are:

1   to develop listening and befriending skills

2   to ensure understanding of the role of befriender and its limitations

3   to help parents come to terms with and understand their own early emotions, prejudices and judgements, and how these might affect the befriending relationship

4   to develop ways of using personal experiences which are sensitive and appropriate to another parent

(Dale and Woolett, 1989, quoted in Cameron and Sturge-Moore, 1990, p. 68).

3.40   If you know of any parent-to-parent schemes in your area, perhaps you can find out how far they are controlled by the professionals, rather than being shaped by the parents themselves.

4   INTEGRATING CHILDREN AND SERVICES

4.1   You have read about the existing range of pre-school services in the United Kingdom and about some of the services provided specifically for young children with disabilities or who experience other kinds of difficulties. Services are provided by statutory authorities, such as health, education and social services departments, by voluntary organizations, such as the PPA or MENCAP, by community groups and by private enterprises. The fragmentation, regional variation and lack of commitment in practice to pre-school provision denies many parents a range of options from which to choose.

4.2   In this section we look at policies and practices aimed at the closer integration both of pre-school children and of pre-school services. Examples of organizations which have attempted to develop overall policies for integrating children include the Welsh Pre-School Playgroups Association and the social services department of the London borough of Islington. One particular playgroup which welcomes children with a very wide range of abilities and interests is the Cirencester Opportunity Group, a voluntary group which exists in a county where there is no nursery education, where most four-year-olds attend primary schools and where most parents of children with disabilities do not have the option of an appropriate service in an integrated setting.

4.3   The section concludes with a discussion of the possibilities of bringing the statutory and voluntary services closer together so that a more unified structure may provide a more flexible service for all young children and their parents. In TV Programme 2, *Learning to Care*, we look at the attempts of one local authority, Strathclyde, to bring together educational, social, recreational and voluntary services for pre-school children within their education department and we examine the implications of this unification for the participation of children with widely varying abilities.

DEVELOPING POLICIES FOR INTEGRATION

4.4   Here we look at two examples of the development of policies for the integration into mainstream provision of children who were previously catered for separately. The first is an attempt to include all children within the ordinary range of pre-school social services in one inner London borough; the second is a plan to include all children within the network of pre-school playgroups in Wales.

Activity 4   Social services for children under five

Now read 'Attempting to integrate under fives: policy in Islington, 1983–8', by Margaret Boushel, Claire Debenham, Lisa Dresner and Anna Gorbach, which is Chapter 8 in Reader 2. As you read, make a note both of the arguments given by the authors for developing a policy of integration and of those given by its critics for preserving a separate specialist system.

Jot down some notes in answer to the following questions:

•   What range of pre-school services existed in Islington during the 1980s? Which of them were designed specifically for children with disabilities or other kinds of difficulty?

- Where did the impetus for change come from and what were the main obstacles? Why did it turn out to be impossible to overcome them?

- In thinking about key people and key events, what, in your opinion, could have made a difference to the outcome of the Islington integration policy? What could have been done to retrieve the situation after 1985? What can we learn from this candid account about the ways in which policies are taken up or are dropped?

4.5   This is mainly the story of a 'bottom-up' policy initiative which did not have the support of vital senior officers and policy-makers. There was resistance to the development of a more generic service from some professionals, who argued that necessary specialist services would be lost in the proposed structure. There was a failure of communication and follow-up discussion at a crucial time, just after the conference 'A place for all our children' had produced a detailed list of recommendations. There were also changes in political priorities, a reorganization of social services across the borough and severe spending cuts imposed on the council. Under-fives were not able to maintain a high profile while all this was going on.

4.6   One sub-theme of the chapter is the link between Islington's strong commitment to an anti-racist policy and a commitment to increasing the participation in ordinary groups and services of children with disabilities or other difficulties.

1989 and after

4.7   Margaret Boushel, Claire Debenham, Lisa Dresner and Anna Gorbach were all working for Islington's social services department between 1983 and 1988, and this is an account of their experiences and perceptions of events during that period. Their careers have now, in the early 1990s, taken them into new jobs in different areas. The Islington story has moved on.

4.8   Since the chapter was written, pre-school provision in Islington has dramatically changed. With the abolition of the Inner London Education Authority in 1988, Islington and several other boroughs decided to take advantage of the fact that educational responsibilities were, for the first time, now conterminous with health and social services responsibilities and set up a structure for under-fives that would co-ordinate the range of services. Under-fives services have been brought together within the education department.

4.9   Staff still working in Islington are cautious about the new system. For example, the day centres, which include many children seen as at risk in various ways, are not now managed by social services but by education and so there is less day-to-day contact between social workers and children than there was before. One day centre has merged with a nearby nursery school, with the ex-headteacher as the officer in charge of the new centre, and it is run very much like a school. While this may be to the advantage of most of the young children, there may be problems for others if the *ad hoc* visits made by health visitors, social workers and speech therapists in the past cannot continue because permission would first have to be sought from the centre's governors. The centre remains open from 7:45 a.m. to 5:45 p.m. all year round, however, and attendance is excellent, better than it was in the day centre. Overall, there are more three- and four-year-olds attending a pre-school centre than before, but fewer under-threes.

4.10   Local authority cuts have meant that two children's day centres have closed, leaving one area of the borough without one. This means that access to education as well as to social services and daycare are inequitably distributed. Further, some of the services provided by non-statutory organizations, such as the Family Service Unit, have disappeared along with their grants. Of the children in each of the new Under Fives Education Centres, it is estimated that about 30 per cent are 'in need', according to the definition contained in the Children Act (1989). (See para. 2.25.) Also, in a fifty-place centre, six places are reserved for children with 'special educational needs'.

4.11   The Beacon Nursery, mentioned in the reader chapter as one of the provisions which triggered discussion about integration in the early 1980s, is still a separate nursery, although in a different building, with about ten children. It looks unlikely, at present, that the children will transfer to the mainstream because the necessary facilities have not been set up for them in the pre-school centres. At the nursery's old building, a new local parents' group, formed because of a mutual interest in conductive education (see Unit 8/9), has organized a two-day-a-week group for children with diverse disabilities.

4.12   What is the situation in your area? Are social services and education still provided separately for children under five or are there moves to bring them together? If so, what facilitated the moves and what were the obstacles? If you have any experience of the social services department in your area, do you think that a similar plan for integration could have evolved? If services are still separate locally, are there any marked differences of policy and approach between education and social services?

Activity 5   Voluntary services for children under five

Now read 'Community play' by Veronica Hanson, which is Chapter 9 of Reader 2. As you read, consider the following questions:

- Where did the policy come from?

- What has made its implementation possible?

4.13   What is noticeable about this story is the coincidence of top-down and bottom-up policies: the Welsh Office and the playgroup movement shared a commitment to integration, the PPA particularly because of their support for parental choice and the government department expressing their view in terms of rights of access and individuality.

4.14   Veronica Hanson talks about 'natural support systems'. Beliefs about what is 'natural' colour most debates about making provision for people with disabilities or who experience other kinds of difficulties, even when these beliefs are not made explicit. Some people have believed that it is 'natural' to segregate those with disabilities, for their own protection or for everybody else's, or to put them with 'their own kind', seeing disability itself as 'unnatural'. These issues will be explored further in Unit 14.

4.15   Veronica Hanson sees pre-school provision as the obvious place to start the implementation of a policy based on human rights. The system should be 'right from the start'.

4.16   Funding can be a problem if you do not want to stress the special difference of people for whom a service is designed, because there will be problems calculating how many people might be involved. There is usually pressure to label client groups very clearly and distinctly. The commitment of central government enabled the Welsh PPA to secure funds without having to go through this negative labelling process. Workers in the playgroups support parents and children when they become involved in formal assessment procedures under the 1981 Education Act, but in a positive way, helping parents to describe their children's capabilities and interests (see also Section 5 for experiences of pre-school assessment).

4.17   This story also represents a two-way collaboration between voluntary and statutory bodies, which has engendered a naturally diverse service.

4.18   Do the playgroups in your own area welcome children with widely varying abilities? If not, why not? If they do, what kind of support makes this possible?

PRACTISING INTEGRATION IN THE ABSENCE OF A POLICY

4.19   In Gloucestershire in 1990, nearly 90 per cent of children under five attended a pre-school group of some kind, but with the voluntary and private sectors as the main providers. There were no local authority nursery schools.

4.20   Glen Cossins, Gloucestershire's advisory teacher for 'Special Needs (Early Years)', set out the main issues which face families with young children with disabilities or other difficulties:

(a) The lack of provision in some areas of the county.

(b) The lack of information about what is available.

(c) Duplication of resources due to lack of co-ordination in policy-making and planning.

(d) Recognizing and providing for a range of parents' and children's needs.

(e) Providing specialist support to children. Can this be done locally? If not, what problems are associated with the children having to travel? How can parents best be involved? How can professionals best be involved?

4.21 A report of the county's Under Fives Review Group recommended that services should be accessible to all children 'wherever they live and whatever their needs' (Gloucestershire Under Fives Review Group, 1990).

4.22 A second review document, *Special and Equal: a whole county approach*, also appeared in 1990 but this was more equivocal about access to ordinary services, partly because of the absence of mainstream pre-school educational provision. The alternatives seemed to be to strengthen the specialist opportunity groups and/or extend the provision in the playgroups, using the opportunity groups as bases for outreach support work. The review recommended extending the role of the playgroups, extending pre-school support in the home and extending 'the amount and range of special provision' (Gloucestershire County Council, 1990, p. 13), thus recommending more of everything but not outlining any clear direction of policy.

4.23 This is the context in which the Cirencester Opportunity Group maintains its independent policy and practice of integration.

The Cirencester Opportunity Group

Activity 6 All together: Cirencester Opportunity Group ———————

Now read 'All together: Cirencester Opportunity Group' by June Statham, which appears as an appendix to this unit. As you read, consider the following questions:

• When and why was the group founded?

• What range of support is available to families which use the group?

• Who benefits?

• Why is the future of the group uncertain and what is the solution put forward by its co-ordinator?

———————————————————————————————

4.24 Many parents across the country see opportunity groups or integrated playgroups as an excellent and 'natural' provision for their children, with or without disabilities. But, as we shall see in Section 5, central government is, in the early 1990s, ambivalent about their value. On the one hand, playgroups are seen as a not very serious form of pre-school provision, catering mostly for children who do not come within any category of 'special need' and who therefore do not require the guaranteed support of the state. Also, playgroups are run, not by professionals, but by untrained or semi-trained parents. On the other hand, playgroups are attended by an enormous proportion of children under five and, in 1989, they cost a tenth of the expenditure on nursery education. So it may make good sense to build up the educational provision in playgroups, although this is the opposite of what was done in Cirencester, where the teacher's salary was transferred to the special school when the qualified member of the playgroup's staff retired. You will also have noted from the case study that the playgroup staff do not relish any increased control by the education authority, despite their willingness to receive a teacher's salary, because they value their independence.

4.25   These debates characterize relationships between government and voluntary pre-school service providers, highlighting the unusually co-operative relationship described by Veronica Hanson between statutory and voluntary services in Wales.

CO-ORDINATION OR UNIFICATION OF SERVICES?

4.26   The existing labyrinth of pre-school services segregates children of parents who work outside the home, and so who cannot make use of nursery schools or playgroups, from children whose parents are freer to use groups which run on a sessional basis. It also segregates children seen to be 'in need' from most of their peers, as provision made for them does not usually cater for the full range of children's abilities, interests and childcare needs.

4.27   People who work in pre-school settings are also divided: teachers, childminders, nursery nurses and playgroup workers have different training, levels of pay and conditions of employment, and they experience different status within the community (Hevey, 1987). Yet they are all working with children and however their particular work setting is designated, it is not possible in practice to separate care, play and learning.

4.28   When a parent, a childminder or a nursery nurse feeds a baby and at the same time holds the baby close and talks to her, this is an experience which promotes physical health, helps to make the baby feel secure and gives her an experience of language. Who is to say that this is either care or education? Surely it is both? And if, in the course of feeding the child, the caregiver uses language in a playful way, unselfconsciously timing speech to the baby's reactions, then care, learning and play go hand-in-hand. Similarly, playgroup and nursery staff provide activities such as jigsaws and painting, which in a school would be called 'educational'. For their part, teachers comfort children when they are upset and clean up their grazed knees and their runny

The Cirencester Opportunity Group.

noses, attending to the children's needs for physical and emotional care. Some staff who recognize the shared nature of their work feel angry that, nevertheless, they do not share an equal status.

4.29   The accreditation of experience, knowledge, skills and practice, whether they are arrived at through training, work or parenthood, will soon be available through the National Vocational Qualification system (NVQ). The system does not, at the time of writing, apply to people who have a professional qualification, for example, nurses, teachers or social workers. What kind of system would redress these inequalities?

4.30   The Children Act (1989) should lead to greater co-ordination at local level as it places a duty on social services and education departments jointly to review childcare services for children up to the age of eight every three years. This new age limit is an acknowledgement that continuity of experience from pre-school to infant and junior school is necessary and that parents continue to require childcare after their children begin full-time education (Petrie, 1986).

4.31   The Act also gives social services departments the power, though not the duty, to seek the help of the local education authority to register and inspect childcare provision. Local authorities are also encouraged to consult and collaborate with the voluntary sector, with parents, private providers and local employers. Guidance on the Act says: 'Coordination is necessary at three levels: policy making, day to day operation of services and between staff working in different settings' (Department of Health, 1991).

Activity 7   Bringing services closer together

Now read 'Provision for the under fives: bringing services together' by Kathryn Riley, which is Chapter 7 of Reader 2. As you read, make a note of the arguments that are put forward for bringing pre-school services closer together. Consider the following questions:

*   Where does the impetus for change come from?

*   What is the difference between 'co-ordination' and 'unification'?

*   What obstacles lie in the way of greater co-ordination or unification and how could these obstacles be removed?

One of the local authorities discussed by Kathryn Riley is Strathclyde, the authority that is the subject of the television programme *Learning to Care*, which you will be watching later as part of this section of the unit.

4.32   Kathryn Riley argues that the demarcations that exist between the different local authority departments that provide services for children under five deny the fact that families' requirements are not separate and would be better met by a more flexible system. There are legal problems for those authorities which do not want to move towards a more unified system and there are difficulties when children under five are given a lower priority in practice (despite the rhetoric of their unique value) because they are a non-statutory group, at least as far as the education authorities are concerned.

4.33   Kathryn Riley confirms that great regional variations exist in the type and extent of pre-school provision and she describes the conflict between national policy and policies in those areas which are keen to develop their network of services.

4.34   Manchester City Council decided not to bring services together within their education or social services departments but to create a separate under-fives department, to reflect the generic nature of the new system that they aimed to develop. Towards the end of her chapter, Kathryn Riley suggests that there should, perhaps, be a department of government solely devoted to the provision of services for children under five. What is your reaction to these proposals? As a way to consolidate a flexible and unified service, then it would seem to be obvious to create a free-standing department. However, as we know, young children are not always given a high priority in practice; many services provided for them are discretionary and, after all, the children do not vote. Might it not be the case that a generic under-fives department would be accorded the same low status as the consumers of its services? Strathclyde Regional Council decided to place its Pre-Five Unit within the high-status education department and award its co-ordinator the rank of assistant education officer.

4.35   Another issue raised by Kathryn Riley is the relative effectiveness of top-down and bottom-up initiatives. How far do innovative policies have the support of both policy-makers and those involved in their implementation?

CARE AND EDUCATION IN STRATHCLYDE

4.36   In Section 2 you read about the variety of services for children under five. These different services have different aims and reflect the different commitments of their organizers and funders. The picture is complicated by the fact that the requirements of parents of very young children for stable and high-quality childcare is seen by some providers as irrelevant to the service they run or even as in conflict with the interests of the children. Where this happens, the relationship between supply and demand may be tenuous. Local government priorities, inter-professional status relationships, the flexibility and the accessibility of pre-school services are all issues which run like themes through discussions of policy-making. Kathryn Riley illustrated some of these arguments in her reader article.

4.37   You have read about the efforts of one particular group of professional workers to develop a more comprehensive service for under-fives. The story of what happened in the Islington social services department illustrates the possibilities and limitations of bottom-up initiatives which do not have the support of senior managers and policy-makers. What can happen when, by contrast, there is a strong central commitment to change?

4.38   In this section we shall examine policy and practice in the Strathclyde region of Scotland, where, in 1986, a Pre-Five Unit was set up within the education department. After looking at the background to the policy, you will be asked to watch TV2, *Learning to Care*.

Background: a major policy review

4.39   In Strathclyde, the impetus for a review of services for pre-school children came from the reorganization of local government and the concern of both councillors and officers about the acknowledged high level of deprivation in the new region. A joint member/officer working party identified a number of problems with the system of pre-school services that existed before 1985.

4.40   As a result of these observations, the working party's final report outlined the following principles for the future development of pre-school services: parental involvement in the planning and running of services should be seen as essential; services should be flexible, locally based and better targeted towards families who required them most; services provided by the education and social work departments of the local authority and those provided by voluntary organizations should all be seen as part of a single network; and co-operation between voluntary and statutory bodies, including the health authorities, should be increased.

4.41   The report discussed whether or not there should be co-ordination or unification of pre-school services and, unlike Manchester, concluded in favour of unification:

> Simply creating coordinating mechanisms between the services does not necessarily work. While some good examples of coordination are apparent, the overall picture remains one of poor coordination between Educational and Social Work with existing hierarchical structures acting more to hinder innovative developments than encouraging them.

> (Strathclyde Regional Council, 1985, p. 21)

4.42   The decision to unify pre-school services within the education department rather than create a separate department was justified in the following way: care and education would be combined and the current professional distinctions be reduced; there would be 'one door' for parents, voluntary and community groups and health authorities; both management and policy development could be more effective in a single department.

4.43   The only people we met who were uneasy about the Pre-Five Unit being sited within the education department were members of the Strathclyde Pre-School Playgroups Association, who felt that their efforts to broaden their service to children and parents were hindered by a traditional disregard of teachers for pre-school groups with a focus on play. Links between playgroups and primary schools have not been good in Scotland and the Scottish Education Department does not provide support for the establishment of playgroups on educational premises, despite falling rolls and the availability of adequate space. Playgroup experience is seen as irrelevant to the child starting school. Some social work professionals have been more sympathetic to the extension of the playgroup network, which, in the rural areas, is the main provider of pre-school services. So some playgroup leaders would have liked to see an independent Pre-Five Unit which they believe would place a greater value on their work.

The Pre-Five Unit

4.44   The unit was set up in 1986, with eight members of staff based centrally in the education department and development officers based in each of Strathclyde's divisional offices. The head of the unit, Helen Penn, was given the status of assistant education officer. The unit's progress report for 1987–8 includes a diagram to show where the unit fits into the structure of the education department as a whole (Figure 6).

4.45   The same report lists the range of pre-school services for which the unit took over responsibility. This is reproduced in Figure 7. You will see that there are great differences between the six divisions of the region, both in numbers of pre-school children and in the nature of existing services. For example, Argyll has practically no statutory services but nearly as many playgroups as Glasgow, which has more than ten times the number of pre-school children.

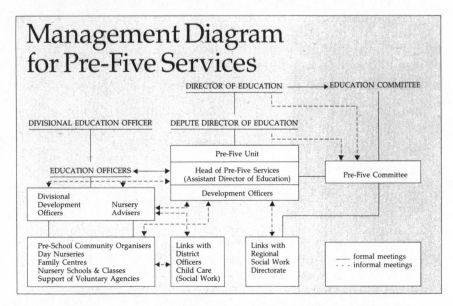

Figure 6 Management diagram for pre-five services (Strathclyde Regional Council, 1988, p. 6).

<table>
<thead>
<tr><th></th><th>ARGYLL</th><th>AYR</th><th>DUNBARTON</th><th>GLASGOW</th><th>LANARK</th><th>RENFREW</th></tr>
</thead>
<tbody>
<tr><td>Nursery Schools</td><td>0</td><td>20</td><td>14</td><td>84</td><td>6</td><td>15</td></tr>
<tr><td>Nursery Classes</td><td>0</td><td>8</td><td>6</td><td>14</td><td>26</td><td>13</td></tr>
<tr><td>Day Nurseries</td><td>0</td><td>3</td><td>2</td><td>19</td><td>1</td><td>6</td></tr>
<tr><td>Family Centres</td><td>0</td><td>1</td><td>2</td><td>9</td><td>6</td><td>10</td></tr>
<tr><td>Resource Centres</td><td>0</td><td>2</td><td>2</td><td>5</td><td>1</td><td>2</td></tr>
<tr><td>Miscellaneous Projects</td><td>3</td><td>6</td><td>6</td><td>32</td><td>13</td><td>6</td></tr>
<tr><td>Link-up Groups</td><td>5</td><td>6</td><td>12</td><td>55</td><td>31</td><td>14</td></tr>
<tr><td>Childminders</td><td>39</td><td>306</td><td>362</td><td>368</td><td>330</td><td>214</td></tr>
<tr><td>Playgroups</td><td>74</td><td>155</td><td>121</td><td>88</td><td>166</td><td>99</td></tr>
<tr><td>Under 5 Population</td><td>3,999</td><td>24,239</td><td>21,303</td><td>44,618</td><td>33,757</td><td>22,961</td></tr>
<tr><td>APTs
(Areas of Priority Treatment)
(accepted by Scottish Office for Urban Aid)</td><td>0</td><td>10</td><td>4</td><td>39</td><td>20</td><td>11</td></tr>
</tbody>
</table>

Strathclyde Regional Council Facts and Figures

Figure 7 Pre-school provision in Strathclyde (Strathclyde Regional Council, 1988, p. 3).

Under-fives with disabilities or other difficulties

4.46   The Strathclyde Regional Council has a Pre-Five Sub-Committee of fifteen councillors. In April 1986, they agreed seven policy principles and in 1987 they added an eighth, referring specially to equality of access to services for children with disabilities:

> Services should be organised in such a way that any provision can accommodate and meet the needs of children with a handicap or chronic illness however severe the condition. The emphasis should be on directing extra resources and support to the community where the child is. No child should be denied access to a service on grounds of health or disability.

> (Strathclyde Regional Council, 1988, p. 16)

4.47   In February 1987, the Pre-Five Sub-Committee agreed a paper presented by the unit and allocated £25,000 to be spent on children with 'special needs' in the financial year 1987–8.

4.48   The unit's policy on disability was seen by its staff as part of its commitment to equal opportunities, but, as their report makes clear, this direction of policy was not yet a central commitment of the council as a whole:

> Strathclyde is an equal opportunities employer, but as yet there is not a high profile given to these issues in the council. The first Race Relations Adviser has recently been appointed to the region. In that context, specific initiatives by the Pre-Five Unit have also been relatively low key.

> (Strathclyde Regional Council, 1988, p. 15; see also Cohen, 1988)

4.49   The member/officer report set its recommendations within the context of limited opportunities for increasing the overall numbers of nurseries in Strathclyde. Therefore, flexibility would need to be achieved by developing services within existing settings, what the report describes as the concept of 'one roof' provision (Strathclyde Regional Council, 1985, p. 29). Local variations were expected to continue but the report recommends: 'a common set of priority admissions in all establishments. These should include ... (c) mentally and physically handicapped children who would benefit from integrating with other children – including those with speech problems' (Strathclyde Regional Council, 1985, p. 33).

4.50   You may notice a difference between the kind of language used by the member/officer group and that used by the staff of the Pre-Five Unit. The use of 'handicapped' suggests the view that the children involved are a separately identifiable group and that their problems do not overlap with those of other children. This attitude is reflected in provision, for, although we filmed in a children's centre which caters for a very wide range of abilities and interests, it was the only one of its kind in Strathclyde. Apart from the Hillend Children's Centre, there are four specialized units for pre-school children aged 0–5 and one nursery class in a special school run by the Spastics Society. Strathclyde is a huge region, so nearly all the children who use these provisions have to travel considerable distances, away from their local communities.

Activity 8   TV2 *Learning to Care*

We filmed in two family centres, one nursery school, one integrated children's centre and a rural playgroup. We talked to parents, policy-makers and professional workers from a range of different backgrounds.

Now watch the television programme. You may have the opportunity to record the programme and so be able to watch it several times.

As you watch the programme, take some notes in answer to the following questions:

- How has the policy of unification been received in practice? Who are its main supporters and who its main critics? How could the criticisms of the policy be answered?

- What are the implications of the policy of unification for the participation of children with widely varying abilities?

- What sort of a pre-school system do you think would best meet the requirements of all families with young children?

4.51   One of the stumbling-blocks faced by the Pre-Five Unit in Strathclyde as they set out to implement a policy of unification was the persistence of professional status-consciousness. People from social work backgrounds were keen to support the changes. They had nothing to lose and everything to gain. They accepted that families might need childcare for a considerable part of each day and wanted to be able to provide a good, all-round, 'flexible' service. If you approve of a scheme, you may well use the word 'flexible'. If you do not approve, you might say that such a scheme would involve 'shift-work', which has quite a different set of connotations. We encountered some revealing use of language as we were making the television programme.

4.52   Education staff feared the loss of identity and status under the new policy, which also represented an assault on the autonomy of the teaching profession. Also, unified pre-school services might cut teachers off from their primary school colleagues, causing discontinuity for both adults and children (see also Section 5).

4.53   One of the most difficult things for a high-status group to accept was that they should consider themselves to be the equals of those other nursery workers whose own educational level was lower than their own. Some felt that this implied both a devaluation of their own educational backgrounds and a trivialization of the reflective approach to their work which they felt characterized 'teaching' as opposed to 'caring'.

4.54   There also appeared to be differences between the adult–child relationships encouraged by teachers and other nursery workers. Teachers usually work with under-fives for short sessions of about two-and-a-half hours. They often work with fairly large groups, compared to workers in 'care' settings, and their focus is on the cognitive, social, emotional and physical needs of the children as 'learners'. Teachers may not be expected to *love* the children in their care. Those who work in day nurseries or other social services, voluntary or community pre-school groups often develop rather different relationships with the children. There may well not be the same amount of curriculum planning as in a nursery school or class, although this will probably change as a result of the Education Reform Act, the Children Act and other official reports on the education of children under five (see Section 5). There may not be many staff who have themselves been through higher education. And there may be a great deal of stress in settings where the majority of the children experience significant difficulties. But, in non-educational settings, there is an expectation that children should be loved, whether or not this is realized in practice.

4.55   These are very difficult, sensitive and intimate issues and therefore hard to discuss with other colleagues. What is your reaction?

Activity 9   True integration?

Children are separated from each other, by perceived ability, by age and by the way in which activities are defined and evaluated by adults. Are any of these separations in the children's interests?

Read these two statements carefully and make some notes in response to each one:

(a) Unifying pre-school education, health, social and voluntary services into a generic system would only emphasize the discontinuity of transferring to school at five and so represent a failure to provide for people's educational lives as a whole.

(b) The apparently irreconcilable split between care and education that characterized the situation in Strathclyde in the late 1980s reflects a traditional mind–body dualism in which education is seen by teachers as an intellectual (and professional) activity requiring a consciousness of thought that is absent from the instinctive, physical (and parental) activity of caring. Combining care and education in integrated pre-school centres therefore involves a change in these deep-rooted, hierarchical views about human nature and the implications they have for a right, or 'natural', way to live.

• What is your own view about segregating young children on the grounds of low educational ability or attainment? Do you think that a selective system can be justified?

• Do you think that the advantages of a more co-ordinated pre-school system outweigh the possible discontinuity at five?

• How would you set about resolving the current split between care and education? Would you want to?

Use your notes to work out what your own basic commitments are and, therefore, what kind of pre-school system you would support.

5 EARLY CHILDHOOD EDUCATION AND THE TRANSITION TO SCHOOL

5.1   In this section we look at the educational legislation and official reports of the late 1980s which set the framework for the 1990s. Children under five are not the statutory responsibility of education authorities, nor is provision for them mentioned in the 1988 Education Reform Act. Parents whose pre-school children have a Statement of Special Educational Needs as a result of a formal assessment undertaken under the 1981 Education Act may therefore find themselves in the position of having educational provision made for their children but in the absence of a network of provision for all children generally.

5.2   We shall look at two official reports on the education of children under five, at some of the responses made by educators to the challenge of devising appropriate curricula, at pre-school assessment procedures and at some of the debates surrounding the practice of including four-year-olds in primary school classes.

5.3   The Education Reform Act of 1988 (ERA) covers post-school provision for young people aged sixteen to nineteen but not pre-school provision for children under five. Nevertheless, two documents were published in 1989 which did focus on the education of young children: first, a report from the House of Commons Select Committee on Education, Science and Arts, *Educational Provision for the Under Fives*; and second, a review from Her Majesty's Inspectorate, *Aspects of Primary Education: the education of children under five*. A commitment to making educational provision for pre-school children remains strong among those groups who advise on the formulation and implementation of policy, but is still lacking from the policy-makers of central government.

5.4   However, although ERA does not explicitly cover pre-school education, there are two main ways in which under-fives are caught up in its arrangements willy-nilly. First of all, the National Curriculum will apply to four-year-olds already in primary school classes because they are not specifically excluded. It was up to the subject working parties to deal with this issue and they did not. The working parties did not routinely include people whose expertise is with children under five, despite being asked to do so by the House of Commons Select Committee, who say in their report: 'We would hope that one of the outcomes of this Report would be a higher awareness at national policy-making level of the importance of advice from early years specialists where policies touch on the nursery years' (House of Commons Select Committee, 1989, para. 5.29, p. xxvi).

5.5   Secondly, the assessment of the educational attainments of all seven-year-olds, whatever form this will eventually take, is bound to influence the curriculum of pre-school education in those settings where pre-school experience is seen as a preparation for compulsory education. For these reasons, those who are concerned both with the training of teachers to work with young children and with the planning of appropriate curricula, have responded to ERA by producing examples and discussions of possible approaches to curriculum development which meet the requirements of the legislation while still reflecting the interests and capabilities of the children. Moreover, bearing in mind the concept of the continuity of provision and care put forward in the Children Act (1989), the idea of educational curricula for children aged three to eight is gaining ground among early childhood educators.

5.6   In her report to the Department of Education and Science on the education of children under five, Margaret Clark (1988) reviewed the position in the 1980s and looked forward to likely changes in the 1990s. Provision for pre-school children had expanded during the 1970s and 1980s, though not as fast as the 1972 government White Paper, *Education: a framework for expansion*, seemed to promise. This expansion led to a concern about what was an appropriate curriculum for the age group as a whole and also to a growing interest in the possibilities for including all children within mainstream settings. A number of large-scale research projects were funded by the Departments of Health and Education and Science (see, for example, DES, 1981) with the aim of informing policy in this complex area which covers statutory, discretionary and voluntary services.

5.7   It was found that there were many children who experience difficulties with speech, language or behaviour in ordinary playgroups, day nurseries and nursery schools and classes (Clark, Browning and Robson, 1982). But children with physical or sensory disabilities or who were experiencing marked difficulties in learning tended to be placed in specialized provisions, including the nursery departments of special schools, which take children from the age of two and which were themselves expanding (see Table 3). Overall, the emphasis was on the language and cognitive development of the children, rather than, as in the 1960s and 1970s when fewer children had been involved, on their social and emotional development (Clark, 1988, p. 255).

Table 3 Numbers of children in special schools, 1976 and 1985.

	January 1976	January 1985
Children in special schools under 5 years		
Full time	4,000	4,000
Part time	1,000	2,000
Total	5,000	6,000
Children in special schools over 5 years	145,000	130,000

Data from: HMSO (1987) *Social Trends*, 17.
(Source: Cohen, 1988, p. 38)

5.8   Mainstream and voluntary services were contracting in the early 1990s, except perhaps for those in the private sector, such as workplace nurseries and private nursery schools. This contraction and the effects of ERA may lead to the maintenance or even expansion of specialized pre-school educational provisions.

AN APPROPRIATE EDUCATION FOR ALL THREE- AND FOUR-YEAR-OLDS

5.9   The House of Commons Select Committee (1989) agreed that pre-school education can 'not only enrich the child's life at the time but can also prepare the child for the whole process of schooling' (para. 2.16, p. x). They therefore recommended in their report, *Educational Provision for the Under Fives*, that nursery education should be provided for all three- and four-year-olds whose parents want it and that subsequent expenditure White Papers should reflect this commitment.

5.10   Meanwhile some kind of priority system would have to operate, but for as short a time as possible, to avoid stigma:

A measure of priority must be given to those with the greatest need. However, such a policy of priority can only be implemented effectively as part of the wider policy of expansion called for above. Otherwise, as several witnesses have pointed out, provision becomes dominated by children who are given places for one special reason or another instead of allowing a proper balance to develop between all groups of children. If a balance is not maintained then the full educational experience will not be available and there is a danger that some form of social stigma will attach to attendance.

(para. 4.27, p. xix; see also para. 7.25)

5.11   The report confirms the value of parental involvement in the pre-school experiences of children and acknowledges that parents play a more active role in playgroups than they do in nursery schools and classes. Playgroups themselves are seen as valuable (see paras. 7.30–7.39) but the report seeks 'to improve the educational content and quality of playgroups' (para. 7.34, p. xxxviii) and recommends that 'the principal responsibility for support for playgroups for older children should be transferred to the DES' (para. 7.39, p. xxxix). Needless to say, the Pre-School Playgroups Association (PPA) was highly critical of both these statements when the report was launched at a press conference in January 1989.

5.12   In her review of the report for *Forum* magazine, Annabelle Dixon (1989) discusses the delicate relationship between the Department of Education and Science and the PPA. She tells us that, at the time she was writing, there were about 267,000 three- and four-year-olds in nursery schools and classes, about the same number again of four-year-olds in primary school but about 600,000 children enrolled in playgroups. The government was expecting to spend £536 million on nursery education in the year 1989/90, whereas the playgroups would cost £51 million. Clearly, it was in the government's interests to collaborate with the PPA, just as it was in the PPA's interests to work with the DES, which might support the movement with a substantial grant. (In January 1992, the DES announced that it had doubled its grant to the PPA from £327,000 to £650,000.)

5.13   The report recommends the closer collaboration between education, social, health and voluntary services and there is a section which describes the advantages and disadvantages of a generic form of pre-school provision (paras. 7.23–7.29). 'Joint centres' can provide a wide range of special services to children and families within a diverse mainstream setting and they can become the base for the continuing education of parents. But they challenge traditional forms of management and organization, they are very expensive and there are difficulties associated with the co-operation between workers from different professional backgrounds. 'Because these Centres do not fit neatly into the pattern of services traditionally provided by the different agencies there is some vagueness in administration, accountability and in the directing of appropriate professional advice' (para. 7.27, p. xxxvi). Referring to a centre in Northamptonshire, the report says: 'for social services it is a problem because it concentrates a lot of resources on a small area to affect a general population rather than a particular population' (para. 7.25, p. xxxvi).

5.14   The report does, however, argue that 'care and education, with the involvement of the parents, must be present in all provision for this age group' (para. 7.29, p. xxxvii) and recognizes that the different pay and conditions of the professionals who work with young children is a major obstacle:

> We recommend that where necessary education and social services departments agree between them pay and conditions for these centres which take into account experience and qualifications but also the particular nature of the provision (for example, that such centres are open, generally, for 50 weeks of the year).
>
> (para. 7.29)

5.15   But the report argues that this development, instead of being an essential feature of pre-school provision in the future, is not needed everywhere: 'We would suggest that where there are fewer deprived children the intensive work with the family which goes on in the combined centre is less of a priority: care and education can be carried out in other ways' (para. 7.29). So the report is 'cautious' about recommending joint centres as 'the way forward generally for under fives provision' (para. 7.29, p. xxxvii), a position which was challenged at the press conference and defended with the argument that the committee was primarily concerned with the curriculum for pre-school children and that its focus was on the children themselves, rather than on the requirements of their parents. Critics at the conference argued that the committee had failed to acknowledge the context of children's real lives and that a universal, generic service, so far from detracting from a high-quality education service, was the only way to ensure its success.

FOUR-YEAR-OLDS IN PRIMARY SCHOOLS

5.16   The report of the HMI on *Aspects of Primary Education: the education of children under five* (HMI, 1989) is the first in a series of reviews of primary education and it is based on inspections carried out between 1985 and 1988. A main reason for including children under five in a discussion of primary education was to examine the effect of the introduction of the National Curriculum on four-year-olds in reception classes. The following figures are adapted from the HMI's report (HMI, 1989, p. 5):

- 45 per cent of under-fives receive education in nursery or primary school classes.

- 24 per cent of this number are in nursery schools or classes.

- 21 per cent of this number are in reception classes of primary school.

5.17   Nearly as many children under five attend primary schools as attend nursery schools and classes. Why is this? I can think of these six reasons. You may be able to think of more.

(a) Falling rolls made space for them and schools were keen to keep their numbers up.

(b) Admission to an existing reception class is cheaper than staffing a new nursery class and much cheaper than building nursery schools.

(c) Any pre-school setting can be seen as providing childcare and as attendance at a primary school can eventually be full-time, this can make it attractive to parents.

(d) Early admission to school may seem to be giving a child an educational flying start.

(e) Admitting children to primary schools at the beginning of the year in which they are five makes for a simpler bureaucratic life for the local education authority.

(f) Children under five are not generally seen as different kinds of learners to those over five.

5.18   The inspectors condemn the practice, despite the numbers involved, and give six reasons why 'children in nursery schools and classes receive a broader, better balanced education than those in primary classes' (para. 6, p. 5):

(a) a curriculum based on play and exploratory activities;

(b) a narrower age-band;

(c) better staff–child ratios;

(d) purpose-built facilities more likely;

(e) more appropriate resources;

(f) appropriately trained teachers.

The inspectors see children under five as different kinds of learners from children of statutory school age. This is a view which derives from a theory about universal child development which stresses the unique importance to young learners of active participation and relevance to their immediate social and concrete experience. Participation and relevance should therefore characterize any early childhood curriculum.

5.19   However, this view can be challenged when the education of young children is set into the context of their educational careers as a whole. For example: Why should children under five be segregated for their education from children over five, even if their learning needs are different? But are they different really? Should not the education of children over five also be characterized by active involvement and relevance? Or would this be to acknowledge that 'play' should have a central place in the education of children over five, with all its connotations of self-direction rather than teacher-direction?

5.20   Moreover, we have discussed in Section 4 the advantages of working towards flexible, better co-ordinated pre-school services. But a generic system, which provides care and education for under-fives in purpose-built or adapted combined centres and which can therefore include children with a diversity of abilities and interests, may find itself cut off from the statutory educational mainstream, thus breaking the continuity of experience for children as learners. These dilemmas remind us how difficult it is to reach agreement about what system would best serve children's interests.

5.21   If the developmental stage of children under five is thought of by the HMI as qualitatively different from that of children over five, this does not mean that they believe that the principles underlying approaches to curriculum planning should also be peculiar to the age group, for, they argue: 'Certain general principles that inform the planning and evaluation of the curriculum for children of compulsory school age hold true for the under fives' (para. 19, p. 9). Perhaps this is a way to build continuity into a system which involves such a chasm at five?

> As for older pupils, the curriculum for young children needs to be broad, balanced, differentiated and relevant; to take into account the assessment of children's progress; to promote equal opportunities irrespective of gender, ethnic grouping or socio-economic background; and to respond effectively to children's special educational needs.
>
> (para. 19)

5.22   As you read Units 6/7 and 8/9 you will be asked to consider whether or not the concepts of breadth, balance, differentiation and relevance are in fact as mutually compatible and unproblematic as they might at first appear (see also 'Hardening the hierarchies: the National Curriculum as a system of classification' by Will Swann, which is Chapter 7 in Reader 1).

5.23   The inspectors recommend that initial teacher training should cover ages three to seven and that students should not be able to specialize exclusively in either the three to five age group or the five to seven age group. The task facing teachers of children under five will be to respond both to the requirements of ERA and to what they see as the developmental requirements of their pupils.

A CURRICULUM FOR THE EARLY YEARS

5.24   Concern about curriculum planning for young children after the passing of the Education Reform Act in 1988 soon resulted in the publication of relevant projects, for example: *Early Childhood Education: the early years curriculum and the National Curriculum* (Early Years Curriculum Group, 1989) and *Working with Children: developing a curriculum for the early years* (Drummond, Lally and Pugh, 1989), a training pack of activities produced by the National Children's Bureau Under Fives Unit.

5.25   The Early Years Curriculum Group was formed in 1988 and one of its aims was to lobby against the mass testing of seven-year-olds and its presumed effects on the education of three- to seven-year-olds. The group saw that the provisions of ERA about the National Curriculum were largely about content and they believed that an awareness of the process and context of young children's learning was essential. They describe the differences between younger and older learners in this way:

> Teachers of young children have to be aware of the development of the whole child as a person. All aspects of the young child's functioning are interdependent and any one can facilitate or constrain the development of ability or attainment. As children grow older it is more possible to consider some functioning as of less immediate concern to the teacher. For example, physical or social needs can increasingly be deferred to the demands of classroom study. In the case of the youngest children, however, it is of critical importance for healthy and productive living and learning that teachers do not lose sight of the general picture in pursuit of detailed information exclusively about what children know and can do in the subjects of the curriculum.
>
> (Early Years Curriculum Group, 1989, p. 20)

5.26   The most substantial section of the *Early Childhood Education* project includes exemplars of 'learning webs', or detailed curriculum plans, for children up to the age of seven in English, mathematics, science and design and technology, which are annotated to show how they relate to the government's standard attainment targets (SATs or ATs). Ideas radiate out from a central topic statement; they are not organized into hierarchies of 'knowledge' (see Figures 8 and 9). They are supposed to be woven around the children's previous experience, their developmental level and their particular interests, which is to say that curriculum planning should be done by those who know the actual children involved.

5.27   The training pack, *Working with Children*, is aimed at teachers, play leaders and nursery staff to work through together in small groups. It contains sections on defining 'learning' and 'curriculum', on the value-systems of those working with children under five, on critical self-reflection, on the observation of current practice and on planning future curricula. The activities are designed to help participants explore their approaches to the curriculum but do not, in themselves, constitute a curriculum plan (see Figures 10 and 11 for some examples). This pack can be seen both as reinforcing the idea that young learners require a particular educational approach and as going some way to implement the proposal contained in the House of Commons Select Committee Report for strengthening the educational content of playgroups.

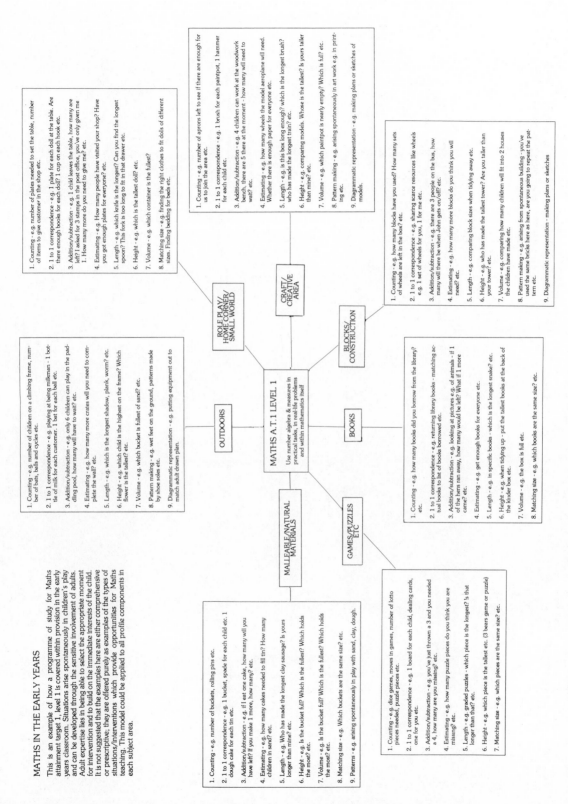

Figure 8 Maths in the early years (Early Years Curriculum Group, 1989, p. 6).

ENGLISH IN THE EARLY YEARS

In developing and extending reading, the importance of communication within a genuine and supportive context is crucial. Print related context can be linked to any topic or story theme where careful observation, reading and recording are appropriate to the child's level of understanding. Telling and reading stories/poems to and with young children provides an enjoyable shared experience at school and home.

Through such a medium they come to realise the existence of printed language, learn to understand the function of print and punctuation and develop and extend their potential repertoire of competency in literacy.

The examples given below are not comprehensive, and should not be seen as prescriptive. They are provided to illustrate some of the opportunities for English teaching which exist in the early years classroom.

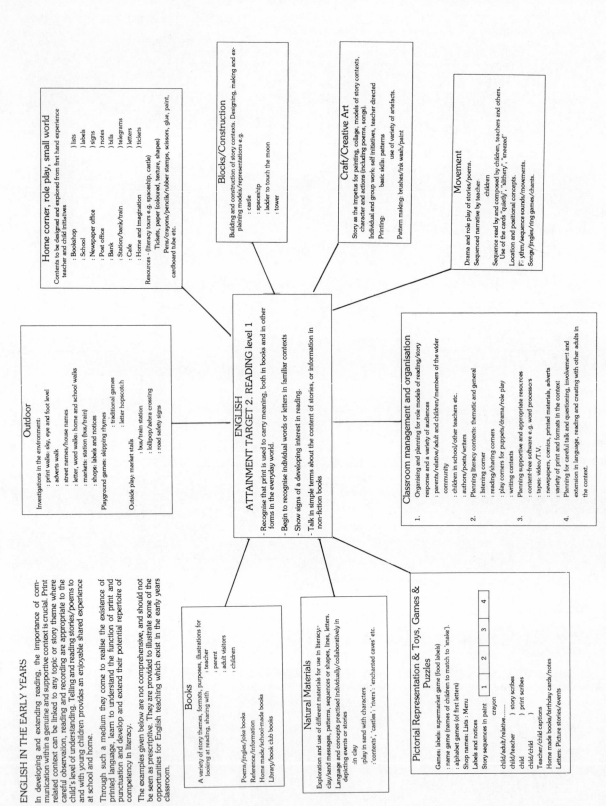

Home corner, role play, small world

Contents to be designed and explored from first hand experience teacher and child initiatives

: Bookshop) lists
: School) labels
: Newspaper office) signs
: Post office) notes
: Bank) bills
: Station/bank/train) telegrams
: Cafe) letters
: Home and imagination) tickets

Resources - (literacy tours e.g. spaceship, castle)
Tickets, paper (coloured, texture, shapes)
Pens/crayons/pencils/rubber stamps, scissors, glue, paint, cardboard tube etc.

Blocks/Construction

Building and construction of story contexts. Designing, making and explaining models/representations e.g.

: castle
: spaceship
: ladder to touch the moon
: tower

Craft/Creative Art

Story as the impetus for painting, collage, models of story contexts, character and actions (including poems, songs).
Individual and group work: self initiatives, teacher directed
Printing: basic skills: patterns
use of variety of artefacts.
Pattern making: brushes/ink wash/paint

Movement

Drama and role play of stories/poems.
Sequenced narrative by teacher.
children
Sequence read by and composed by children, teachers and others.
Use of the cards "quietly", "slithery", "sneezed"
Location and positional concepts.
Fi ythm/sequence sounds/movements.
Songs/jingles/ring games/chants.

Outdoor

Investigations in the environment:
: print walks: sky, eye and foot level
: adverts walk
: street names/house names
: letter, word walks: home and school walks
: markets: station (bus/train)
: shops: labels and notices

Playground games: skipping rhymes : traditional games
: letter hopscotch

Outside play: market stalls
: bus/train station
: lollipop/zebra crossing
: road safety signs

ENGLISH
ATTAINMENT TARGET 2. READING level 1

- Recognise that print is used to carry meaning, both in books and in other forms in the everyday world.
- Begin to recognise individual words or letters in familiar contexts
- Show signs of a developing interest in reading.
- Talk in simple terms about the content of stories, or information in non-fiction books

Classroom management and organisation

1. Organising and planning for role models of reading/story response and a variety of audiences
: parents/relative/adult and children/members of the wider community
: children in school/other teachers etc.
: authors/poets/writers

2. Planning literacy contexts: thematic and general
: listening corner
: reading/sharing corners
: play corners for puppets/drama/role play
: writing contexts

3. Planning supportive and appropriate resources
: content-free software e.g. word processors
: tapes: video/T.V.
: newspapers, comics, printed materials, adverts
: variety of print and formats in the context

4. Planning for careful talk and questioning, involvement and extension in language, reading and creating with other adults in the context.

Books

A variety of story themes, formats, purposes, illustrations for looking at: reading, sharing with : teacher
: parent
: adult visitors
: children

Poems/jingles/joke books
Reference/information
Home made/school-made books
Library/book club books

Natural Materials

Exploration and use of different materials for use in literacy:- clay/sand messages, patterns, sequences or shapes, lines, letters.
Language and concepts practised individually/collaboratively in depicting events or stories

: in clay
: play in sand with characters
: 'contexts', 'castles': 'rivers': 'enchanted caves' etc.

Pictorial Representation & Toys, Games & Puzzles

Games: labels: supermarket game (food labels)
: name game (names of children to match to snake).
: alphabet games (of first letters)
Shop names: Lists : Menu
Labels and notices

Story sequences in paint | 1 | 2 | 3 | 4 |
crayon
child/adult/relative......
child/teacher) story scribes
child) print scribes
child/child
Teacher/child captions
Home made books/birthday cards/notes
Letters: Picture stories/events

Figure 9 English in the early years (Early Years Curriculum Group, 1989, p. 5).

54

7. CURRICULUM GUIDELINES FROM LOCAL AUTHORITIES

The publication of *Curriculum Matters 2*, the Education Reform Act of 1988, papers from the National Curriculum Council and developments in the social services sector, have led many local authorities to produce written guidelines for services for young children. These are varied in content and it would be impractical to attempt to summarise them. The most useful approach is to look at the guidelines produced in your area and/or for your service and consider some of the questions in Activity 7D.

Activity 7D

EXAMINING LOCAL GUIDELINES

Time 30 - 60 minutes (or longer, depending on guidelines)

PREPARATION
Each member of the group will need to have read the local guidelines. If education and social services departments have produced separate guidelines, it might be worth looking at both.

ACTIVITY

In groups of three and four discuss the questions below.

1.   Do the guidelines have an underlying philosophy? Is this philosophy spelled out or left implicit? In such a philosophy what emerge as the needs of children, of families, of services and of those who provide the services?

      Look back to section 6. Do the values of such a philosophy seem to be consistent with your values?

2.   Do the guidelines appear to have been influenced by any of the major schools of thought on curriculum?

3.   Do the guidelines assume that all children are the same or is there specific recognition of cultural differences?

4.   Do the guidelines talk only of he or of she, or assume gender-related patterns of play or use of play materials?

5.   What is left out? For example, do the guidelines assume a particular age range of children? Of training and/or experience of staff? Do they assume a particular pattern of relationship with parents?

6.   What are the implications of the guidelines for you? If you and your colleagues were responsible for implementing the curriculum in the guidelines what would it mean for you in time, energy, reorganisation, questioning of your assumptions?

IN WORKING THROUGH THIS SECTION YOU WILL HAVE

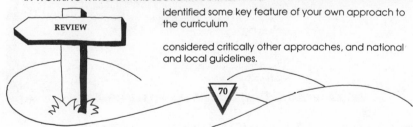

identified some key feature of your own approach to the curriculum

considered critically other approaches, and national and local guidelines.

Figure 10 Approaches to the curriculum (Drummond, Lally and Pugh, 1989, p.70).

Activity 7A

A CHILD'S EYE VIEW   Time 45-60 minutes

PREPARATION
Before the group discussion in this activity, each participant should observe and keep a diary of how a particular child spends a day or half a day.

NOTE TO GROUP LEADERS
If group members are working in very different settings there may be a tendancy to get bogged down in unimportant details. Members may need encouragement to concentrate on questions of WHY and HOW?

ACTIVITY

1 Working in pairs, discuss your observations of how a child responds to the curriculum you are offering.
What have you learned about
> the child?
> your curriculum?
> yourself?

2 Think about the whole session from the child's point of view:
> the learning environment in and out of doors, including organisation of space and resources
> the daily routine and activities
> interactions with adults

3 In groups of three to four, ask

> *what provision* do you make in each of those areas?
> what choices are available?
> what choices did the child make?
> to what extent did the adults influence decisions?
> what were the child's experiences of different size groups?
> how was the time divided between different activities?
> *why* do you do or provide the things that you do?
> *what* do you hope the children will learn or achieve?
> *how* do you know the children are learning or achieving?
> i.e. how do you evaluate what you are offering the children?
> *which* aspects of your approach are you most/least satisfied with?

Figure 11 Activity 7A, a child's eye view (Drummond, Lally and Pugh, 1989, p. 54).

Assessing children's educational needs

5.28   To plan appropriate curricula staff need to know about the experiences, interests and abilities of the children with whom they will be working. Under the terms of the 1981 Education Act, children may have their educational needs assessed at any time from birth onwards. The process may be initiated by the health authority, the educational authority or the parent. The Act places a duty on education authorities to identify, assess and provide for children with 'special educational needs' aged between two and sixteen. For children under the age of two, assessment can be carried out but only with the consent of the child's parent. The Department of Education and Science Circular 1/83 says: 'Early education is of crucial importance for young children with disabilities. The Secretary of State for Education and Science hopes that LEAs will continue to give priority to children with special educational needs in admitting children to nursery schools and the nursery classes of primary schools' (see Newell and Potts, 1984, p. 1).

5.29   Assessment under the 1981 Education Act involves gathering advice from a psychologist, a doctor, other relevant professionals, such as a speech therapist, a health visitor or a teacher, as well as a contribution from the child's parent, whose views are to be taken seriously and who is to be fully involved and consulted at every stage of the assessment. For children over five who have been through the formal assessment procedure and have been identified as having 'special educational needs', the education authority has a duty to prepare and review a 'statement' of these needs. For children under statutory school age, there is no duty placed on the education authority to make a statement following an assessment. However, all children in segregated educational provisions are supposed to have a statement and many special schools have nursery classes which take children from the age of two, so this group should all have a statement. Also, parents who want an integrated placement for their children when they start at nursery school or playgroup may see the possession of a statement as one way to secure any necessary additional support for their child, as this support can be specified in the statement, which, in theory at least, has the status of a legal document which should be honoured.

5.30   The Fish Report (1985) on special educational provision in the Inner London Education Authority describes how stressful the assessment process can be for parents:

> There was general anxiety (and much misconception) amongst parents about the purpose and nature of assessment for children under five. We were told that the education welfare officer, who delivered the letter informing parents that 'formal assessment' procedures were to be started, sometimes did not stay long enough

to answer any questions. Most parents were unsure about the purpose and nature of their contribution to the Statement and extremely confused about the purpose of the examinations.

Many parents found the apparently random, and often isolated, examinations by people they did not know confusing and apparently bearing no relationship to each other.

…

There was considerable disquiet about the outcome of assessment, namely appropriate provision, particularly where a child is attending social service, voluntary or health services provision. When delays occur, staff and parents become disillusioned and are reluctant to see assessment as purposeful and relevant.

Parents thought that they were given inadequate information about the options for provision after assessment. Most felt that they needed simple and readable information on all relevant provision, with opportunities for an encouragement to make visits.

(ILEA, 1985, p. 47, paras. 2.6.10, 2.6.11, 2.6.16, 2.6.17)

5.31   The Fish Report recommended that assessment be undertaken as a continuous exercise, with professionals going to the child's home or nursery and that time be spent by professionals making sure that the parents' own needs for information and support are also met. Those parents who have been involved in some form of pre-school provision and who have had the experience of working with their children alongside a professional are obviously in a better position to formulate their own views and voice them strongly.

5.32   Linda Jordan has written about her daughter's assessment in this way:

By the time Ellen was two, we had decided to ask for her 'special educational needs' to be assessed under section 5 of the 1981 Education Act. We thought that it was necessary to go through this procedure because we believed that Ellen's needs should be defined and the educational provision she needed should be formally recorded. We did not want the available special education provisions to determine what sort of school Ellen would go to nor did we want her to be permanently 'on trial', as she would be if she went to the local nursery school without a statement.

(Jordan and Wolfendale, 1986, p. 19)

5.33   Ellen, Linda and Chris, Ellen's father, had worked with a Portage home teacher since Ellen was ten weeks old, which 'meant that we were able with confidence to write our contribution to the statement' (Jordan and Wolfendale, 1986, p. 20). Here is what Ellen's parents wrote about her abilities and interests when she was two:

Ellen is two years and two months old. She was diagnosed at birth as having Down's syndrome. When she was four weeks old we

58

were told by a Newham paediatrician that because she was severely mentally handicapped she would be eventually going to a school for severely educationally subnormal children. At the time we did not question this placement, but we have come to do so gradually over a period.

Ellen's motor development has been slow, but with the help of physiotherapy and Portage she walked at 19 months and is now able to climb stairs unaided, walk backwards, and is beginning to run.

She can name a large number of pictures in books and in photographs, both nouns and verbs, and as far as we can tell, her cognitive development is level with that of many two-year-olds who are not severely mentally handicapped.

Her social skills are in advance of what is usually expected from a non-handicapped two-year-old.

Ellen has been able to feed herself and drink from an open cup from the age of 15 months. She asks to go to the toilet. She is clean 90 per cent of the time and dry 50 per cent. She can partly dress and undress herself, imitates drying herself, combing her hair and cleaning her teeth.

Her expressive language is developing at a much slower pace than would usually be expected of a non-handicapped two-year-old. However, she has been learning the Makaton signing vocabulary and uses about 40 signs. She has used more signs, but often drops them when she is able to say the word. She pronounces ten words fully and clearly, and a further 30 incompletely. She will try to say any word which is introduced to her, and has just started to put two words together, usually combining a Makaton sign with a spoken word. At the moment her receptive language skills seem to be a long way ahead of her expressive skills.

Ellen's development so far has led us to the conclusion that it is different from the development of children who are not severely mentally handicapped, and that it is not correct to describe it as 'retarded'. Apart from the area of expressive language, her achievements are similar to those of non-handicapped children of her age. However, the *route* to her achievements has been different, and has required different kinds of input. She does not learn 'automatically', as other children seem to do at this age, and more things have to be taught to her directly or over a longer period of time. But this is balanced by the fact that she is more amenable to teaching than many non-handicapped children.

This is a contribution to Ellen's statement and therefore has the purpose of establishing her learning difficulties. In our view her learning difficulties are only 'difficulties' in the sense that they are different from the common types of difficulty which can occur with most other children.

Ellen's needs are:

- She needs to learn how to fulfil a role in life both now and after she leaves school, and to be a happy, participating member of her community.

- She needs to be accepted as a human being with full rights, not someone to be laughed at or feared.

- She needs to be included in a full range of activities alongside her peers.

- As a means towards exercising these rights, she needs to develop her physical, communicative, logical, artistic, musical, practical and social skills as far as possible.

None of these needs is special, since they are taken for granted in the case of the vast majority of children. They are only 'special' in Ellen's case because fulfilment of them is usually denied to severely subnormal people, and because she may require more resources in order for them to be met than is usually the case. What is special is the provision needed, and we consider the following special educational provision to be necessary for the time being if Ellen's needs are to be met:

1   Placement in her local neighbourhood school (St Stephens Nursery School) where she will receive the stimulation that she needs from her peers. The authority's normal practice, as revealed to us when Ellen was born, would be to place her in Beckton School nursery class. It is clearly impossible to meet the first three of the above needs if she is segregated from her peers and her local community. Section 2(2) of the 1981 Education Act states that where an authority arranges special educational provision for a child for whom it maintains a statement, it has a duty to secure that he or she is educated in an ordinary school. We can therefore see no grounds for Ellen to be denied the placement we are asking for.

2   The staff who will be in most immediate contact with Ellen need to understand the nature of her condition and the general way in which her development differs from the norm.

3   This staff may need to acquire some knowledge of the Makaton signing vocabulary.

4   This staff will also need to understand how to catch and hold Ellen's attention, and to get used to the speed at which she reacts to events, verbal instructions, etc.

5   There must be extra close liaison between home and school, so that Ellen's time at home can be used to reinforce what she is doing at school.

6   We expect that Ellen will continue to need speech therapy. However, we see no reason why this should not continue to take place under the present arrangements rather than in school.

(Jordan and Wolfendale, 1986, pp. 29–31)

5.34   Ellen started at her local nursery school when she was four but she continued to receive the support of her home liaison teacher, Pauline, who had been working with Ellen since she was three and who had accompanied Ellen on visits to the school during the term before she began attending. Pauline worked with Ellen in addition to the Portage home teacher.

5.35   Parents whose children are involved in a pre-school service can benefit in two ways when it comes to writing out their own views of what their child can do and what he or she 'needs' educationally. Firstly, the pre-school worker can help in the preparation of a parent's contribution. You will remember from your reading of the article by Veronica Hanson about the Special Needs Referral Schemes in Wales that playgroup leaders will support a child's parents in the preparation of their contribution to a statement by helping them to describe their child's interests and behaviour. Secondly, the experience of working together can give a parent the confidence that their views are indeed vitally relevant: 'Our contribution turned out to be more comprehensive and detailed than any of the professional advice written about our daughter. This bears out my belief that parents who work with their children become "experts"' (Jordan and Wolfendale, 1986, p. 20).

A special curriculum?

5.36   In her book *Pre-school Provision for Children with Special Needs*, published in 1989, Brenda Robson sets her discussion of appropriate curriculum planning for children with widely varying abilities within the context of the aims of nursery education as a whole: 'The overall aims of nursery education must be applicable to children with special needs. The objectives of the nursery curriculum must be fully stated to reflect these aims and to be relevant to the needs of all children' (Robson, 1989, p. 21). Robson is critical of the 1981 Education Act for referring to the activities of the ordinary classroom without feeling the need to refer to the aims and objectives from which they derive. She says that this omission is common, that there is a reluctance clearly to define what a nursery curriculum should be, stemming partly from a lack of consensus on the value of pre-school education.

5.37   Vital to curriculum planning is the need to understand how children learn. Brenda Robson describes Piaget's theory of child development and emphasizes the need for children to be actively and concretely involved if they are going to learn. The implications for children with physical or sensory disabilities are that, as there will be limits to their abilities to engage in exploratory activities, there may be gaps in their cognitive development. Appropriate curricula for young children with physical disabilities, therefore, must aim to fill in these gaps. For children who experience difficulties in learning, who may be described as being 'developmentally delayed', the curriculum just needs to be flexible enough to cope with a varied pace. Where children are seen as experiencing 'gaps' or 'delays', adult intervention is implied.

5.38   Brenda Robson makes a number of points which relate to the nature of the social relationships between teachers and learners in pre-school settings. First of all, it appears that some children may need support to get started and to be able to enjoy and persist in play activities, and that they may benefit from the continuing participation of an adult. However, 'Staff are very reluctant to become involved in fantasy play. If they do take part, they tend to dominate the interaction rather than facilitate' (Robson, 1989, p. 45). Brenda Robson sees that there is a taboo here, that staff find playing with children for any length of time difficult. Is this because it is plain embarrassing or because it means acting like the parents they do not want to substitute for? Or is this kind of involvement with children on their own terms in fact seen as unprofessional, not part of the job of an observing and self-reflecting nursery worker?

5.39   Secondly, Brenda Robson notes that many young children experience difficulties of communication and that this has definite implications for extended interactions with adults and in the context of the children's play rather than within adult-directed learning activities:

> The debate about the relative importance of play and work in the nursery is purely semantic, since no meaningful distinction can be made in educational terms between the two concepts in relation to pre-school activities … [Staff] should be able to interact actively with the children at all levels of play, thereby encouraging sustained participation and concentration and the development of more complex patterns of play. As well as contributing directly to the children's learning and cognitive development, the staff will be encouraging children to relate to each other and will be learning much more about the children as individuals, this being a crucial aspect of ongoing assessment and planning.
>
> (Robson, 1989, p. 50)

RISING FIVE

5.40   Transferring to school at five is a momentous experience for any child, but there are exceptional stresses for some children and their parents. The Fish Report, for example, listed a lack of information passing between provisions and between the local authority and families, bureaucratic delays, inexperienced staff, poor liaison between relevant professionals, parental anxiety about the negative labelling consequences of formal assessment at rising five and pressures from over-worked professionals for families to accept placement decisions that they themselves felt were not sufficiently thought out. Perhaps the idea of . remaining in one special school for an entire educational career from two to sixteen or even nineteen begins to tempt at this stage? Some of the most active parents' groups in the United Kingdom were formed when a number of families in an area were faced, for the first time, with the prospect of a full assessment under the 1981 Education Act, together with the need to make a decision about the kind of educational experience they wanted for their children as they approached statutory school age.

5.41   Brenda Robson argues strongly against any inclination on the part of receiving schools to give the incoming children a 'clean slate', agreeing with the Inner London parents and staff that full and up-to-date information is essential (Robson, 1989, p. 144). She also notes that some children may be transferring to schools at a greater distance from their homes than will be the case for most children, indicating that pre-visits by child, parent and pre-school staff are especially important. One of the problems for all children when they transfer to the next phase of education is that parental involvement becomes successively harder to maintain, requiring great persistence from parents. Keeping in close touch with your child's school may be more difficult if that school is a long way away, if you do not regularly take your child to school in person and if the school does not reduce these difficulties by circulating adequate information and by creating as many opportunities for involvement as possible. Finally, Brenda Robson argues for flexible admissions policies and against admitting children with special needs to primary school before they are five.

Activity 10   Pre-school education

If you are not the parent of a pre-school child, imagine you are. What sort of educational experience would you want for your child? Reflecting on what you have read in this unit and in the reader, considering the TV programme *Learning to Care* and making use of your own experience and that of children known to you, make a list of those factors that seem to you to be relevant and important. Spend about twenty minutes working on this.

Now imagine you are an early-childhood educator. What sort of experience would you want to secure for all pre-school children in your area? Again reflecting on the course materials and on your own experience, spend about twenty minutes listing the factors that seem to you to be relevant and important.

Compare your responses to the above two paragraphs. Do they reveal any differences in perspective? If so, how could they be reduced or responded to creatively?

6   CONCLUSION: RIGHT FROM THE START

6.1   This unit has been concerned with exploring ideas about making appropriate provision for children under five. Setting children's social and learning experiences within the full context of their present and future lives is a necessary complication for service providers if children are going to be able to make the best use of provision.

6.2   The three main issues which have arisen from this discussion of children under five seem to be:

- First, what should a pre-school system consist of? How can a more secure and comprehensive pre-school system be developed? What is the place of specialist services within such a system?

- Second, how can the split between 'care' and 'education' be amended? How can disability and uncertainty about its causes and effects be accepted as part of ordinary life?

- Third, should there be legislation to make pre-school education mandatory? Should there be a minister to take responsibility for putting the high-priority rhetoric about children under five into practice? Should the law be changed to make it easy to establish generic under-fives committees at local government level?

A POLICY FOR CHILDREN UNDER FIVE?

6.3   Here are four expressions of support for the development of a central policy for children under five. First, the HMI report on the education of children under five recommended that the Department of Education and Science should extend its responsibilities to cover three- and four-year-olds in playgroups (HMI, 1989, para. 7.39, p. xxxix). Secondly, in her review of this report, Annabelle Dixon argues that: 'only when there is proper recognition in terms of ministerial responsibility and possibly a coordinating minister for this age group, will there be power enough to enforce the recommendations on the range and quality of provision and the essential training of staff and monitoring of standards' (Dixon, 1989, p. 74). Thirdly, in her reader article, Kathryn Riley concludes that 'only a major change of heart from central government' will enable committed local authorities to implement their policies and oblige the rest to pay attention to the needs of young children. Finally, discussing the current legal difficulties faced by local authorities who want to set up under-fives council committees, Gillian Pugh of the Under Fives Unit at the National Children's Bureau argues that: 'a problem in developing local policies is the lack of any clear directives from central government … there is legislation which empowers or enables local authorities to provide services, but no statutory requirement and no overall national framework to guide development at a local level' (Pugh, 1989, p. 67).

6.4   The House of Commons Select Committee was discussing the education of children under five at the same time as the Education Reform Bill was being discussed in Parliament, yet there was no mention of pre-school education in the Education Reform Act. Why was this opportunity overlooked?

7 INVESTIGATIONS

7.1 Suggestions for pursuing your own enquiries have been included in the unit as they have arisen, but here are four ideas set out in a little more detail:

Yellow Pages

7.2 Can you find out what range of pre-school provision exists in your local authority? They could encompass:

Social services provisions
Educational provision
Health services
Playgroups
Nurseries run by community groups, commercial enterprises etc.
Home visiting services
Childminding
Other voluntary services
Other play provisions
Toy libraries
Local childcare campaign
Local branch of the National Childbirth Trust
Etc. …

You could seek information from: the library, education, health or social services offices, the town hall, GPs, the telephone directory, community centres.

- Are services part-time, full-time, day-time, residential?

- Is there a directory of pre-school services already published in your area? If so, does it include the full range of services? If not, what does it leave out?

- What provisions welcome children with disabilities or other difficulties? Which do not? Which services are designed exclusively for these children?

7.3 If there isn't a directory, could you make a start on compiling one?

What do families want?

7.4 Are there any organized parents' groups in your area? If so, are you yourself a member? If not, ask if you can attend a meeting or arrange another time to visit the group and talk to them about how and why they got together. Perhaps you could tape-record a short conversation between three or four parents, or otherwise take some notes. You could try to find out:

- What issues have top priority for these families?

- What are their short- and long-term aims?

- What kinds of experiences have brought them together?

- What does the group do?

- How does the group support and fund itself?

- What changes in local policy and practice can be attributed to the activities of the group?

Pre-school services in action

7.5   See if you can arrange to observe a session in one of the following: the Child Development Centre, a local playgroup or a private home while a home visiting teacher is working with a child and his or her parent. Choose a setting that is unfamiliar to you. If you could undertake your observations in collaboration with a friend or colleague and, also, visit more than one kind of provision, then you will find that you have much more material to compare and discuss. But half a day spent in observing what goes on in one setting will provide you with ample food for thought.

- Decide how you are going to record what you see and hear and what role you are going to play while you are in the session. Will you participate or not? Will you be able to avoid participating, whether you like it or not?

- How would you like to present your interpretations of what you record? How could your findings be useful?

A policy for children under five

7.6   Interview the people responsible for making and implementing policies for pre-school children in your area, politicians and workers. Choose to focus on health or education or social services, unless these have already been brought together in your area.

- Is there a written policy statement and, if so, does it reflect a clear commitment to a particular direction of change or does it simply argue for more of everything? If there is no document, ask why not.

- If there is a policy statement, ask your interviewees about the difficulties they have encountered putting that policy into practice and how they have tried to overcome them.

- What do your interviewees think about bringing 'care' and 'education' closer together?

- Do they believe that only children seen to be 'in need' should be provided for at the public's expense or do they believe that all families who want to use pre-school services should have equal access?

- What do they see as the advantages and disadvantages of partnerships between themselves and other statutory authorities and between themselves and voluntary or commercial organizations?

- Do your local politicians support the proposal that there should be legislation to extend the duties of the Department of Education and Science to include children under five?

APPENDIX   ALL TOGETHER: CIRENCESTER OPPORTUNITY GROUP

June Statham

INTRODUCTION

Gloucestershire is a large rural county which traditionally has low levels of pre-school provision. There is no local authority nursery education attached to ordinary schools; instead children start school early, entering reception class in the September after they become four. In the whole county there are eighteen local authority family centres, fourteen run by education and four by social services. The voluntary and private sectors play a very important role in under-fives provision, with an estimated 70 per cent of Gloucestershire children attending a pre-school playgroup before they start school.

For children with disabilities or who experience other difficulties, the options depend very much on where in the county they happen to live. There is a small Portage project, involving parents and children in their own homes, which provides for around twenty families in the Gloucester town area. There are seven opportunity centres run by the local authority which offer part-time places to children aged two to five with a variety of disabilities or other perceived needs. Some of these sessions are only for these children; others offer opportunities for the children to mix more widely. There are also seven nursery classes/assessment groups attached to special schools which children may attend from the age of two. Most of this provision is located in the major towns, such as Gloucester and Cheltenham, so many children have to travel a long way from home.

Although pre-school provision for the majority of Gloucestershire children is a voluntarily-run playgroup in their nearest village or town, this is not the case for children with disabilities. The local authority recently instigated a review of services for children identified as having special needs which reported that although 'arrangements can be made to help playgroups to take part in the process of identifying children with special needs and assessing them, and subsequently to support the children … they are not generally resourced for these purposes and such arrangements are relatively rare' (Gloucestershire County Council, 1990).

CIRENCESTER OPPORTUNITY GROUP

However, there is one playgroup in Gloucestershire which does welcome pre-school children with disabilities or other kinds of difficulties and which can draw on specialist services and resources for support. The Cirencester Opportunity Group describes itself as an 'independent integrated playgroup enabling children with special needs to play and learn alongside other children from the community'. It was set up in 1973 by a mother whose own child the local playgroup had earlier refused to accept. She founded the Cirencester group to help mothers in a similar position to herself but this was after her own son's pre-school year. From small beginnings, opening two mornings a week in a church hall, the group has grown and in June 1984 moved into its own purpose-built premises with a playroom, parents' room, staff office, kitchen and outside play area. The money for this was raised over five years by a huge fund-raising effort in the local community, and the building was erected with MSC labour.

The playgroup children

Half the children in the playgroup have a disability or difficulty of some kind. In the past, the group has included children with spina bifida, cystic fibrosis, Down's syndrome, diabetes, and hearing difficulties, while other children have experienced social difficulties or difficulties in learning. A child from the local area will always be offered a place and the playgroup tries to keep one or two places vacant in order to be able to respond quickly to emergencies, but children without disabilities or who live further away often have to go on to a waiting list because of the demand. Over the last few years, the children themselves have changed, so that there are currently few children in the opportunity group with physical disabilities but more who experience problems arising from their social circumstances or who experience difficulties in learning. This could be because there are fewer children with severe difficulties being born in the area, or it could be because some of these children are being channelled towards the nearest special school, which over the last five years has been developing its nursery programme.

Many children are referred to the opportunity group by doctors, health visitors, speech therapists or social workers. The playgroup aims to be able to accept any child, whatever their difficulty, and if necessary the supervisor will call on extra voluntary help, either to work directly with the child or to allow a more experienced member of staff to do so. The supervisor has a pool of volunteers that she can call on in such circumstances, although the trend towards more women going back to paid work means that this supply is diminishing.

Children usually join the opportunity group at the start of the term when they become three, but children with disabilities may be admitted from the age of two. The playgroup is allowed to take up to twenty children a session but tries to keep this down to around sixteen, both to give a better adult–child ratio and also to provide the flexibility to take new children at short notice. It offers four mornings, from 9:15 a.m. to 1:00 p.m., including lunch, and two afternoon sessions a week, with the afternoons mainly reserved for younger children and the mornings for those nearing school age. Most children can only attend two playgroup sessions a week because of the demand for places, although children with disabilities or other kinds of difficulties may be offered three or four sessions, or indeed may stay all day, according to the circumstances. There is also a parent-and-toddler group held on Tuesday afternoons and Wednesday mornings, and a family session on Wednesday afternoons to which parents can bring both toddlers and older pre-school children. A holiday playscheme for children up to age six is held during part of the summer holidays.

Children usually stay in the opportunity group until starting primary school in the September after their fourth birthday. Most go on to their local school, including those with disabilities or who experience other kinds of difficulties, but a few go instead to the special school in the area or move on to specialized units attached to schools in Gloucester or Cheltenham, some miles away. The opportunity group leader liaises with the local schools. Reception staff come to visit the group and playgroup children go out to visit the nearest infant school, where most of them will go in due course.

There are also links with the local special school nursery and sometimes children transfer there after their time in the opportunity group. In rare circumstances a child might spend part of their time in the special school nursery and part in the opportunity group. Staff co-operate closely when this occurs. This arrangement is not encouraged by the playgroup, however, as staff feel that the confusion caused by two environments for a child who is already experiencing difficulties is neither necessary nor in the child's best interests.

The workers

There are currently three paid workers running each playgroup session, the teacher/supervisor and her two assistants. They are supported by volunteers and, usually, a parent helper, though the parents' rota is not compulsory. Many of the volunteers are regular helpers who have been assisting with the group for many years. Most live locally, like working with children and support the aims of the group. Some have had children of their own attend the group in the past. One young woman with learning difficulties who lives in a sheltered housing scheme and spends most of the week at an adult training centre, has been helping in the playgroup two days a week for over five years now. In addition to the staff who work directly with the children, the playgroup employs an administrator, cook and cleaner.

Management and specialist support

The opportunity group is a registered charity managed by a committee of parents, volunteers and friends, who are jointly responsible for maintaining the building, fundraising and employing staff. An advisory group of professionals meets once a term with members of the committee and staff to advise on playgroup policy and they can be called upon for any specialized help or information. There is a close involvement with the Pre-School Playgroups Association (PPA) and both staff and parents attend courses run by the local branch. The PPA Foundation Course, in particular, is considered to be essential for staff. The local authority pre-school advisory teacher is also a regular visitor to the group.

A speech therapist refers children to the group and comes in once a week to work with children and to liaise with staff. The physiotherapist visits regularly when a child in the group needs this support and other professionals, such as the teacher for the deaf and the clinical medical officer, also visit to assist staff and assess children as necessary.

The playgroup supervisor finds this support extremely useful:

> We get excellent back-up from the professionals. I can ring up the physiotherapist any time to ask her advice, or call in the child psychologist to work with a whole family. I get invited on the local authority's INSET training courses, on topics like counselling and working with parents of children with special needs. The head of the hearing impaired service came here to train our staff and helpers when a particular child who had a hearing loss was a member of the group last year.

A TYPICAL MORNING

On a typical morning, there are about sixteen children in the playgroup. Most are brought by their parents. On Monday mornings a few stop to have a coffee and talk over any problems with a regular volunteer in the parents' room, which also has a window on to the playroom enabling parents to watch their child in the group without being observed. Some children from outlying villages are brought in by a transport scheme which was originally funded by a government Opportunities for Volunteering grant. This money has now run out, but a core of volunteers with cars still collect and take home children who need a place but are unable to get to the playgroup.

The children spend most of the morning in a well-equipped playroom. Different activities are laid out on small tables, such as shape-matching games, Lego, paper and crayons, cutting and sticking and dough. There is a home corner with rag dolls and toy telephones; an indoor climbing frame and slide; easels and tables for painting on; a sand tray and another for water play; and a small library room opening off the main playroom containing children's books, small tables and chairs, large floor cushions and a full-length child-sized mirror. The toilets are easily accessible and well-designed for a variety of toileting needs, with child-sized toilets and wash-basins, large sinks, a changing area and a special toilet adapted for adults who use a wheelchair. The building has its own outside play area, both grassed and paved, with sand pits and outdoor equipment such as balancing planks, frames, balls and wheeled toys.

Children are free to choose what they do, assisted by the supervisor, her two assistants and two volunteer helpers. The theme today is 'long and short', and while some children roll long and short sausages of coloured dough, others paint pictures on long and short pieces of paper or string beads into different sized necklaces. During the morning children can help themselves to a snack; some arrive without any breakfast and need to eat before they can concentrate on playing. Before they leave all the children are given a hot lunch, cooked on the premises and served at small tables in the playroom. The meal not only gives parents a longer break from their children, it also offers a useful opportunity for the staff or visiting professionals to work with the children on any feeding difficulties or other dietary needs that they may have.

Before lunch the children all gather together to listen to a story, sing songs and perform action rhymes. The workers may need to use Makaton, a simple sign language used alongside speech, to help those children who experience difficulties in understanding or hearing speech. Language development is seen as important for all children and the educational aims of the group are the same for everyone, whatever their abilities and interests. The environment of the group is designed to foster all aspects of development: intellectual, social, physical and emotional. Particular attention is paid to the encouragement of listening and concentration skills.

SIMON

Sometimes children need special equipment to enable them to participate fully in the playgroup, and this is often loaned by the health authority. Simon, a child with spina bifida who has now left the opportunity group and gone on to an ordinary school, needed a different sized chair to allow him to sit at the table with the other children, another with sides to keep him upright so that he could have his hands free to play, and a low sand table which his trolley chair could be driven underneath. Whenever Simon was not in his trolley chair, it proved a great attraction to the other children who all wanted to try it out. The physiotherapist also provided large foam wedges for him to lie on so he could play with toys on the floor. The playgroup itself bought a two-child rocking boat which all the children enjoy, but which is particularly useful for giving children like Simon a chance to join in physical play with another child, safely strapped into his side of the boat.

A range of professionals needed to see Simon (ear and eye specialists, dietician, physiotherapist, speech therapist), and the opportunity group provided a link between them. The physiotherapist and speech therapist each visited Simon in the playgroup once a week. The group also provided practical and emotional support for his parents. When they decided they would like an independent medical assessment of Simon, the opportunity group supervisor accompanied the family to Oxford, and she also provided a report herself for Simon's statement of special needs.

Simon started attending the mother-and-toddler group with his mother when he was nine months old, at the suggestion of the family's health visitor. He began at the playgroup at two, initially for two afternoons a week. The playgroup assistant took on responsibility for assisting him with feeding and toileting, and making sure he could participate in all the activities. For Simon's mother, the opportunity group was the obvious place for him to be.

> There was another playgroup on the road we lived in, but he'd been going to the mother–toddler group here and we knew it worked well. The mother–toddler group leader was also the welfare person in the playgroup so they knew all about him. They were prepared to have him, they're the only people that *wanted* to have him. Most playgroups wouldn't have taken him on the grounds that he's not toilet trained. Also we didn't want him labelled and put in a corner. Here he was never excluded from anything, even if it meant him being literally carried around.

Simon's mother had wanted him to attend an integrated, local service rather than the playgroup for children with special needs at the hospital in Cheltenham.

> I wanted him to mix in with everybody and not be channelled off. It would have meant travelling out of the area. If we're in another town, especially if he's in his wheelchair, people often turn and stare. If we go round town here, people say 'Hello Simon' – he's always lived here, and everyone knows him.

FUNDING: THE DIFFICULTIES OF STATUTORY–VOLUNTARY COLLABORATION

The local authority is less supportive when it comes to funding the opportunity group than it has been in providing professional advice. The group receives no regular grant, and is currently operating at a substantial loss. Annual expenditure is around £23,000, but income from parents' fees, fundraising and donations amounts to less than £19,000 now that a three-year grant from the government's Opportunities for Volunteering scheme has ended. The playgroup is having to draw on its reserves, but cannot do this indefinitely. The charge of £1.90 a session, which includes a hot lunch, is very reasonable. Fees are reviewed and increased annually, but raising the fee to match the costs would put the group out of the reach of many who need it most and the management group refuses to do this. The social services department pays the fees of children who have been formally referred to the group, but there are many more whom a health visitor or social worker merely suggest could benefit from a place, who are not sponsored in this way. In fact of the £1,642 paid in fees for children with special needs in 1990, only £250 was given by Gloucestershire social services, and the rest was sponsored by a local charitable trust.

Cirencester Opportunity Group has received local authority funding in the past, but the tangled history of this illustrates some of the potential pitfalls for collaboration between statutory and voluntary sectors. When the founder member wanted to leave to go back into properly paid teaching work she and another teacher-trained worker were asked instead by the local authority to continue running the opportunity group on a teacher's salary, which the LEA would pay. This arrangement worked well until the original founder retired and the funding for a teacher's salary was withdrawn.

The unique nature of the job, which combines the responsibilities of teacher, supervisor and co-ordinator, has no local authority counterpart. The current teacher/supervisor has a strong commitment to the group and had already been working there as a volunteer before being appointed as officer-in-charge. The low salary which the group itself could offer was therefore acceptable and she has now run the playgroup for the past five years.

The three-year grant from the Opportunities for Volunteering scheme cushioned the impact of funding the teacher's salary for some time, but the present teacher is now about to leave as she is moving from the area and the committee is concerned that the advertisement of the post has generated an initial response but no serious applications because of the low wage.

The committee feels that it is important to have a well-trained person in the post, as it is a responsible job and involves substantial liaison with local authority professionals, but they are at the moment unable to offer an appropriate salary.

After their previous experience, however, the playgroup committee is wary of local authority money which has too many strings attached. They want to retain their independence and with it their right to hire staff and decide which children attend. The supervisor says that the great strength of the group is its community basis. Not only are parents very involved, in fundraising, helping in sessions or using the drop-in facility but other members of the local community also support the playgroup. Businesses in the town provide small donations, local people come in to put up shelves, mow the grass, ferry children from outlying villages or tend the garden. As a small, local venture the supervisor feels that the playgroup is better placed to respond to changing needs than a large, bureaucratic organization. The major review of under-fives services which has just been undertaken by the local authority has recommended greater support for voluntary and community initiatives and the supervisor hopes that this may lead them to a system of 'contracting out' some of their services to the voluntary sector, so that the opportunity group could retain parent control whilst also having a more secure funding base.

It is not only the parents of children with disabilities or other difficulties who value the integrated service offered by the opportunity group. The playgroup is popular with many parents, not only because of its longer hours, its attractive purpose-built premises and the provision of lunch, but also because it gives non-disabled children the opportunity of mixing with children they might not otherwise meet. One mother explained why she had chosen the opportunity group for her own two children:

> Some people don't send their children here because they think it's all retarded children. If you meet someone in the park and say your child goes to the opportunity group they sometimes look at you funny. But I think it's a brilliant place. They get the dinner, there's a holiday scheme, the building is very good. And I want my children to grow up knowing what these other children are like and that they're not 'funny'.

For many children in Gloucestershire, integrated provision such as this group is not an option. Children have to travel many miles to attend specialist pre-school services in one of the major towns, whilst those without such needs are deprived of the chance to learn and play alongside children of differing abilities. Offering local provision would mean providing on a much grander scale the kind of support given to Cirencester Opportunity Group by professionals such as physiotherapists and speech therapists, and offering more training and support to playgroup workers. The council's Under Fives Review Group has proposed a goal of integrated provision on a local basis within the next five years (Gloucestershire Under Fives Review Group, 1990), but has yet to develop concrete proposals for how this might be put into practice. In a large rural county such as Gloucestershire, centralization of services and resources can seem the most efficient option. Cirencester Opportunity Group offers a model of community-based integrated pre-school provision which other children and parents in Gloucestershire may have to wait some time to enjoy.

ACKNOWLEDGEMENT

I should like to thank Angela Aldred, the Cirencester Opportunity Group's co-ordinator, for her hospitality, co-operation and detailed comments and advice on the drafting of this case study.

REFERENCES

CAMERON, J. and STURGE-MOORE, L. (1990) *Ordinary Everyday Families ... a human rights issue*, London, MENCAP.

CAMERON, R. J. (ed.) (1986) *Portage: pre-schoolers, parents and professionals*, Windsor, NFER/Nelson.

CLARK, M. (1988) *Children Under Five: educational research and evidence*, final report to the Department of Education and Science, London, Gordon and Breach Science Publishers.

CLARK, M., BROWNING, S. and ROBSON, B. (1982) *Pre-school Education and Children with Special Needs*, report of a DES funded project, University of Birmingham, Department of Educational Psychology.

COHEN, B. (1988) *Caring for Children: services and policies for childcare and equal opportunities in the United Kingdom*, report for the European Commission and Childcare Network, London, Family Policy Studies Centre.

CO-OPERATIVE EDUCATIONAL SERVICE AGENCY (1976) *Portage Guide*, Co-operative Educational Service Agency.

DALE, N. and WOOLLETT, C. (1989) *Parent Support Link Scheme Training Manual*, London, KIDS Family Centre, Camden.

DALY, B., ADDINGTON, J., KERFOOT, S. and SIGSTON, A. (eds) (1985) *Portage: the importance of parents*, Windsor, NFER/Nelson.

DEPARTMENT OF EDUCATION AND SCIENCE (1981) *Under Fives: a programme of research*, handbook published by the Under Fives Research Dissemination Group, London, DES.

DEPARTMENT OF HEALTH (1991) *Children with Disabilities*, Consultation Paper Number 23, London, Department of Health.

DESSENT, T. (ed.) (1984) *What is Important about Portage?*, Windsor, NFER/Nelson.

DIXON, A. (1989) 'Buttering the parsnips', *Forum*, **31** (3), Summer 1989.

DRUMMOND, M.-J., LALLY, M. and PUGH, G. (eds) (1989) *Working with Children: developing a curriculum for the early years*, London, National Children's Bureau.

EARLY YEARS CURRICULUM GROUP (1989) *Early Childhood Education: the early years curriculum and the National Curriculum*, Stoke-on-Trent, Trentham Books.

GLOUCESTERSHIRE COUNTY COUNCIL (1990) *Special and Equal: a whole county approach*, Gloucestershire County Council.

GLOUCESTERSHIRE UNDER FIVES REVIEW GROUP (1990) *Under Fives Review*, Gloucestershire County Council.

HALL, D. (ed.) (1989) *Health for All Children: a programme for child health surveillance*, Oxford, Oxford University Press.

HER MAJESTY'S INSPECTORATE (HMI) (1989) *Aspects of Primary Education: the education of children under five*, London, Department of Education and Science.

HEVEY, D. (1987) *The Continuing Under-fives Muddle: an investigation of current training opportunities*, London, Voluntary Organisations Liaison Council for Under Fives (VOLCUF).

HOGG, C., KOZAK, M. and PETRIE, P. (1989) *Childcare Links: partnership in the community*, London, DayCare Trust.

HOUSE OF COMMONS SELECT COMMITTEE ON EDUCATION, SCIENCE AND ARTS (1989) *Educational Provision for the Under Fives*, Volume 1, London, HMSO.

INNER LONDON EDUCATION AUTHORITY (1985) *Educational Opportunities for All?*, London, ILEA (the Fish Report).

JORDAN, L. and WOLFENDALE, S. (1986) 'Experiencing Portage: an account by a parent and a home teacher', in CAMERON, R. J. (ed.) *Portage: pre-schoolers, parents and professionals*, Windsor, NFER/Nelson.

MENCAP UNDER-FIVES PROJECT, LONDON DIVISION (1986) *A London Directory of Services for Families and their Young Children with Special Needs*, London, MENCAP.

MOSS, P. (1990) *Childcare in the European Community, 1985–1990*, Brussels, European Commission Childcare Network.

NATIONAL ECONOMIC DEVELOPMENT ORGANIZATION (NEDO) (1989) *Defusing the Demographic Timebomb*, London, NEDO Books.

NEWELL, P. and POTTS, P. (1984) *Under-5's with Special Needs. Pre school children: the new law and integration*, London, Advisory Centre for Education (ACE).

NFER/NELSON (1987) *Portage Early Education Programme Checklist*, Windsor, NFER/Nelson.

PETRIE, P. (1986) *After School and in the Holidays: the responsibility for looking after school children*, Thomas Coram Research Unit Occasional Papers 2, London, University of London, Institute of Education.

POTTS, P. (1983) *Integrating Pre-school Children with Special Needs*, London, Centre for Studies on Integration in Education (CSIE).

PUGH, G. (1989) *Services for Under Fives: developing a co-ordinated approach*, London, National Children's Bureau.

ROBSON, B. (1989) *Pre-school Provision for Children with Special Needs*, London, Cassell.

RUSSELL, P. (1990) 'Introducing the Children Act', *British Journal of Special Education*, **17** (1), pp. 35–7.

SHEARER, D. and SHEARER, M. (1986), in CAMERON, R. J. (ed.) (1986), *Portage: pre-schoolers, parents and professionals*, Windsor, NFER-Nelson.

SMITH, J., KUSHLIK, A. and GLOSSOP, C. (1977) *The Wessex Portage Project: a home teaching service for families with a pre-schoool mentally handicapped child*, Southampton, University of Southampton, Wessex Health Care Evaluation Research Team.

STEPHENSON, S. (1990) 'Promoting interaction among children with special educational needs in an integrated nursery', *British Journal of Special Education*, **17** (2) (research supplement), pp. 61–5.

STRATHCLYDE REGIONAL COUNCIL (1985) *Under Fives*, final report of the member/officer Working Group, Glasgow, Strathclyde Regional Council.

STRATHCLYDE REGIONAL COUNCIL (1988) *Pre-Five Unit: Progress report 1987–88*, Glasgow, Strathclyde Regional Council Department of Education.

THE OPEN UNIVERSITY (1989) P558 *The Children Act, 1989: putting it into practice*, Milton Keynes, The Open University.

TIZARD, B. (1986) *The Care of Young Children: implications of recent research*, Thomas Coram Research Unit Occasional Papers 2, London, University of London, Institute of Education.

WHITE, M. (1986) 'Using and developing the Portage teaching materials' in CAMERON, R. J. (ed.) (1986) *Portage: pre-schoolers, parents and professionals*, Windsor, NFER-Nelson.

WHITTINGHAM, V. (1991) *Full Marks for Trying: a survey of childcare provision*, London, Daycare Trust.

ACKNOWLEDGEMENTS

Grateful acknowledgement is made to the following sources for permission to reproduce material in this unit.

Text

Jordan, L. and Wolfendale, S. (1986) 'Experiencing Portage: an account by a parent and a home teacher', in Cameron, R. J. (ed.) (1986) *Portage: pre-schoolers, parents and professionals*, NFER-Nelson

Figures

Figures 1 and 2 The maps are copyright Charlie Owen, Thomas Coram Research Unit, Institute of Education, University of London. They were drawn with the GIMMS computer package. The boundary data are copyright the Department of the Environment

Figures 3 and 4 NFER-Nelson (1986) *Portage Early Learning Programme Checklist*, NFER-Nelson

Figure 5 Adapted from Jordan, L. and Wolfendale, S. (1986) 'Experiencing Portage: an account by a parent and a home teacher', in Cameron, R. J. (ed.) (1986) *Portage: pre-schoolers, parents and professionals*, NFER-Nelson

Figures 6 and 7 Strathclyde Pre-Five Unit (1988) *Progress Report 1987–8*, Strathclyde Regional Council Department of Education

Figures 8 and 9 Early Years Curriculum Group (1989) *Early Childhood Education: the early years curriculum and the National Curriculum*, Trentham Books

Figures 10 and 11 Drummond, M. J., Lally, M. and Pugh, G. (eds) (1989) *Working with Children: developing a curriculum for the early years*, National Children's Bureau/NES Arnold

Tables

Table 1 CEC, 'Children in the European Communities, 1985–1990', from *Women in Europe*, August 1990, Commission of the European Communities, Brussels

Table 2 House of Commons Select Committee on Education, Science and Arts (1989) *Educational Provision for the Under Fives*, reproduced with the permision of the Controller of Her Majesty's Stationery Office

Table 3 Cohen, B. (1988) *Caring for Children: services and policies for childcare and equal opportunities in the United Kingdom*, report for the European Commission's Childcare Network, Family Policy Studies Centre

Photographs

Courtesy of the Centre for Studies on Integration in Education

E242: UNIT TITLES

Unit 1/2   Making Connections

Unit 3/4   Learning from Experience

Unit 5   Right from the Start

Unit 6/7   Classroom Diversity

Unit 8/9   Difference and Distinction

Unit 10   Critical Reading

Unit 11/12   Happy Memories

Unit 13   Further and Higher

Unit 14   Power in the System

Unit 15   Local Authority?

Unit 16   Learning for All